WOMEN IN BLACK

AGAINST VIOLENCE, FOR PEACE WITH JUSTICE

T0243437

CYNTHIA COCKBURN
and SUE FINCH

Fernwood Publishing
Halifax & Winnipeg

Published in the UK in 2023 by Merlin Press Ltd
ISBN 978-0-85036-784-3

Printed and bound in Canada

Fernwood Publishing
2970 Oxford Street, Halifax, Nova Scotia, B3L 2W4
and 748 Broadway Avenue, Winnipeg, Manitoba, R3G 0X3
www.fernwoodpublishing.ca

Fernwood Publishing Company Limited gratefully acknowledges the financial support of the Government of Canada through the Canada Book Fund and the Canada Council for the Arts. We acknowledge the Province of Manitoba for support through the Manitoba Publishers Marketing Assistance Program and the Book Publishing Tax Credit. We acknowledge the Nova Scotia Department of Communities, Culture and Heritage for support through the Publishers Assistance Fund.

Library and Archives Canada Cataloguing in Publication
Title: Women in Black : against violence, for peace with justice / Cynthia Cockburn and Sue Finch.
Names: Cockburn, Cynthia, author. | Finch, Sue (Women's rights activist), author.
Description: Includes bibliographical references.
Identifiers: Canadiana (print) 20230505716 | Canadiana (ebook) 20230505759 | ISBN 9781773636412
  (softcover) | ISBN 9781773636535 (PDF)
Subjects: LCSH: Nashim be-shaḥor (Organization : Israel) | LCSH: Peace movements. | LCSH: Women—
  Political activity. | LCSH: Feminism.
Classification: LCC JZ5578 .C63 2023 | DDC 303.6/6—dc23

MIX
Paper | Supporting responsible forestry
FSC
www.fsc.org
FSC® C013916

WOMEN IN BLACK

CONTENTS

Dedicated to the memory of Cynthia Cockburn
1934-2019

FOREWORD

This book tells the story of Women in Black and explains why it is important: how a network of women committed to peace with justice grew to oppose injustice, war, militarism and other forms of violence across the world and actively speak truth to power.

Women in Black (WiB) is not an organisation, but a formula for action. Reflecting on the inherent violence of militarised patriarchy over the years, the actions and the bravery of these women have inspired many generations in their determined resistance to the continuum of male violence and its ramifications.

Cynthia Cockburn from Women in Black in London started writing this book in 2018 but sadly died in 2019 before she could complete it. Some women from the UK completed the remaining chapters, adding many more stories from across the world. But the movement is continually evolving, and we can only apologise if there are WiB groups and events that have been missed.

Building on the work and aspirations of previous generations, their stand — and their critique — has spread from country to country and continues to develop in different ways in over sixty countries.

This is a history of a movement that must be acknowledged, and preserved, to continue to inspire future generations working against violence, and for peace and justice.

ACKNOWLEDGEMENTS

There are so many Women in Black who helped bring this book together that it has been impossible to thank everyone, but heartfelt thanks to all of you and above all to:

Cynthia Cockburn, who planned and wrote most of this book, and inspired WiB in London and across the world, as well as her wonderful daughters and granddaughters.

Siân Jones for rescuing and organising the UK chapter and advising on everything. Liz Khan for writing her story, the backbone to the UK chapter, and advising on the WiB Armenia chapter and so much else. Rebecca Johnson for contributing to the UK chapter, especially in relation to the 2021 Treaty on the Prohibition of Nuclear Weapons, and throughout the book.

Adriana Medina Lalinde for wonderful translations and checking draft chapters with Spanish-speaking WiB in many countries.

Lieve Snellings for her warmth, international coordination of WiB, constant advice, and amazing photos, together with Ria Convents, both creative WiB activists in Belgium.

Lepa Mladjenović and Staša Zajović for their extraordinary and influential campaigning and peace-making work as WiB Belgrade (*Žene u Crnom*).

Corinne Kumar for taking WiB to India and beyond, creating the powerful Courts of Women, and making a difference to everyone she meets.

Lameez Lalkhen for writing about WiB South Africa and displacement.

Elisabetta Donini, Renata Rovere and Marianita De Ambrogio for their contributions about WiB (*Donna in Nero*) in Italy.

Arpi Balayan and Sonya Hovakimyane from WiB Armenia for their interviews, fearless activism and campaigns in the face of bitter adversity.

Nouritza Matossian, writer, broadcaster, human rights activist, and Honorary Cultural Attaché for the Armenian Embassy in London from 1991–2000, for summarising relevant Armenian history.

Morgan Stetler for preparing the logo for the front cover.

Anne Beech for initial editing, and our fantastic publishers Tony Zurbrugg and Adrian Howe at Merlin Press.

Cynthia Cockburn demonstrating against nuclear weapons at Faslane in Scotland, 2006
© Lieve Snellings

INTRODUCTION

In February 2019, Cynthia Cockburn wrote:

> I have been invited by members of the network to write a history of Women in Black and describe the present reality. The objective of such a book is to further our cause — in brief, to eliminate violence against women and to end militarism and war. We believe that the book will help to make Women in Black (WiB) better known, disseminate its message and attract more adherents. Another objective is to re-state and advance feminist understandings of gender in relation to violence and war.
>
> WiB is already over thirty years old. People pass away and memories fade. It is important to gather and present the historical material before it is too late.
>
> Rape, femicide and the social exploitation of women are endemic. Feminist activism to end gendered oppression and violence is urgent and will be strengthened by fostering a greater understanding of the masculinist and patriarchal nature of militarism and war, and making the scope and extent of current movements for change better known.
>
> Outbreaks of armed conflict are frequent worldwide, between states, and between governments and their opponents. Recently, besides, the threat of armed violence within countries between groups of opposed ideologies, identities and cultures is increasing.

Global military spending — currently more than two trillion dollars a year — is steadily growing. Massive national military budgets squander resources that could and should be spent on people's health and wellbeing. It is urgent to give information about ways of protesting against this and drawing more citizens into activism.

It is also urgent that men adopt, and women support, forms of masculinity that are not shaped by violence and militarism.

Cynthia Cockburn wrote this introduction in February 2019 but died on 12 September 2019 before she finished the book. In the meantime, she wrote five chapters. Given the outbreak of yet more armed conflict in Israel Palestine, Afghanistan, Ukraine, Armenia and elsewhere in 2022, and ever-growing rape statistics across the world, her introduction feels more urgent, and even more relevant, now.

Just before she died, Cynthia asked me to finish the book, gave me the first five chapters and handed over 20 box files of information to include in the remaining two chapters: one on WiB UK, and one on WiB Armenia. As a result, the style of these two chapters had to change from the personal, fascinating narrative of the original five to more collective accounts. Cynthia was a wonderful writer of many books, so this was a daunting task. Luckily, WiB from across the world added their stories, helped to check what was already written for accuracy and contributed to this book.

Women in Black acts across five continents for peace and justice and against violence, militarism and war. WiB's most consistent action is the street-side vigil, positioned at a busy location and repeated at regular intervals. Vigillers wear black, mostly maintain silence and display boldly worded political messages.

Many WiB take more direct action too, demonstrating against war, militarism, murder and rape, using imaginative street theatre and blockading roads that lead to nuclear testing and bomb assembly sites.

WiB has different names in different countries and contexts, depending on the particular focus of the local group: Women in Black against War, Women in Black against Violence and Women in Black for Peace with Justice. We are not an organisation, but a network connected by an international website, international conferences and shared theories, inspiration and actions.

Characteristic and particularly influential country groups of WiB feature in this book, which recounts unique developments, dramatic events and key personalities:

Chapter 1 tells how Women in Black began in Israel in 1988, prompted by the Palestinian intifada, or uprising, of late 1987, with an appeal to 'End the Occupation of the West Bank and Gaza'. This chapter begins with the conflictual relationship between the state of Israel and Palestinians in its historical context, and the inequality and injustice of gender relations in highly militarised Israel Palestine. We see WiB evolving a complex and productive partnership of Jewish Israeli women with Israeli Palestinian women and Palestinian women in the Occupied Territories.

Chapter 2 has three distinct parts, as we see WiB getting under way in the countries to which it first spread:

In the USA, only six months after women in Jerusalem enacted their first WiB vigil, Jewish women peace activists began mounting similar actions in US towns and cities. We trace the rapid and effective development of the Jewish Women's Committee to End the Occupation of the West Bank and Gaza (JWCEO) and growth of WiB in the USA.

a. Italian feminist activists first made contact with WiB in the late eighties when visiting Israel Palestine in the context of a project they called 'Visiting Difficult Places'. We see how they joined Israeli WiB in peace actions and, on returning home, began vigils in Rome, Perugia and other cities under the name *Donne in Nero* (DiN). The chapter draws on a survey DiN carried out, which generated thoughtful reflections by Italian women on the meaning of silence and wearing black.

b. In turn, Italian women travelled to Federal Yugoslavia to support women struggling for peace in that disintegrating state, and inspired feminist activists in Belgrade to create *Žene u Crnom protiv Rata* (*ŽuC* — Women in Black against War). *ŽuC* used WiB methods to fine effect in struggling against Milošević and protesting the Bosnian and Kosovo wars of the 1990s. They internationalised WiB by publishing a series of books in English, Spanish and Italian as well as Serbo-Croat, and organising nine international WiB conferences.

Chapter 3 looks at the antecedents and inspirations for WiB in the UK — starting with the Women's International League for Peace and Freedom, the women's peace camp at Greenham Common, then WiB Belgrade, and moving through protests against the Iraq war in 1991 to weekly silent vigils and non-violent protests against the occupation of Palestine, the wars in Afghanistan, Iraq and Syria, the arms trade and the UK's nuclear missiles, as well as in support of refugees and asylum seekers and opposition to environmental catastrophe.

Chapter 4 pursues the theme of connection and comm-unication within Women in Black. Connecting with WiB in former Yugoslavia inspired women in Spain and Belgium to start WiB groups, as well as a communication network that connects and spreads WiB ideas across the world. Both *Mujeres de Negro* (WiB) in Spain and WiB Belgium continue to lead international coordination of the network.

Chapter 5 shows WiB associating its feminist opposition to war with two related causes — justice for women and responses to displacement — and how their messages adapted to each other.

Justice for women: the Indian feminist Corinne Kumar met Gila Svirsky from WiB Israel Palestine in 1992 and carried the vigil practice back to her home town, Bangalore. Corinne was already part of *Vimochana*, a collective whose main campaigning issue is ending the endemic domestic, sexual and social violence against women. The 16th WiB biennial international conference, was hosted by *Vimochana* in Bangalore in 2015, with a 'Court of Women' attended by over 1,000 people calling for justice of women.

Responses to displacement: the last section of chapter 5 brings us to WiB's 17th international conference, held in Cape Town, South Africa, in 2018. Attended by more than a hundred women from sixteen countries, it was organised by women's groups whose main concern was the impact on South African women of displacement due to slavery, colonisation, armed conflict, poverty and apartheid.

Chapter 6 begins with the active Women in Black movement in Colombia, home to one of the world's most sustained and impassioned women's movements against violence and war. The organisation which gave rise to WiB in Colombia is *La Ruta Pacífica de Mujeres por la Negociación de los Conflictos* (Women's Peaceful Road for the Negotiation of Conflicts), *La Ruta Pacífica* or RPM for short. It is with their story that this chapter on WiB's spread from Europe to South America opens, then extends to Uruguay, Argentina and Chile.

Chapter 7 ends with a group of young WiB in Armenia organising an international WiB conference in Yerevan — introducing new forms of protest like flash mob dancing for peace in public squares. Could this give us hope for the future?

The theories that underpin Women in Black

Women in Black activists are motivated and informed by theories about the relationship between gender and violence, in peace and war. Violence, militarism and war are gendered phenomena, and peace activism, to be effective, must likewise be gender analytical and gender aware.

> Gender relations are lived in all societies to a greater and lesser degree as patriarchal. Men and masculinity are relatively dominant and relatively militarised. Rape is

endemic in peacetime and a pronounced element of war strategies. Economic class structures and ethno-religious cultures intersect with these inequalities, to different effect in different places. (Cynthia Cockburn, 2019)

Theories about the causal relationships between gender and militarism, and the continuum of male violence from the home to the military, evolved as feminists who became part of Women in Black moved between the war-torn spaces of Israel/Palestine and Yugoslavia and visited each other across borders and conflicts.

Cynthia Cockburn describes how, in the early days of Women in Black, *Žene u Crnom* activists in former Yugoslavia began 'a startlingly clear and explicit conceptualisation of nationalist and militarist ideologies and social structures as vehicles of patriarchy, and of women's bodies as pawns in these interlocking power relations' (Cockburn 2007:100).

WiB Belgrade created powerful anthologies of writings about *Women for Peace,* recording a series of international workshops and conferences that influenced developments in theory and practice from 1993 onwards. These were published on international women's day each year, and widely distributed and discussed among Women in Black.

The anthologies bear witness to the anti-war theories and activities of women in former Yugoslavia, working across different sides of the conflict, and the feminists from Spain, Italy, France, Belgium, Chile, Germany, the UK, Canada and the USA who worked in solidarity with them. The *Women for Peace* series developed theories about rape as a war crime, ethnic cleansing, and feminist anti-militarism, and has been reprinted by Women Living Under Muslim Laws (*Femmes Sous Lois Musulmanes*) in France.

From their standpoint, as women face to face with militaristic violence, they perceive a 'sexual division of war' that involves close links between masculinity and militarism. As feminists they understand gender to be a relation of differentiation, inequality and power, founded on violence. Applying this understanding to their life experience, as women in the midst of war, or citizens of countries that source war or profit from others' wars, they perceive gender power relations as an important factor predisposing societies to war, in short as a cause of war. (Cockburn, 2012:9)

Building on these theories, Cynthia argued that 'gender relations were causal in militarisation and war, as well as leading to gendered continua of violence' (Cockburn, 2010:148); these have become central theories for Women in Black.

A feminist analysis is not a bad place to stand to get a perspective on violence as a continuum — from domestic violence (in and near the home) to military violence (patrolling the external boundaries against enemies) and state violence (policing against traitors within). (Cockburn, 1998:44)

At the same time, a theory of transversal politics was emerging out of interactions between Israeli, Palestinian and Italian women connecting across borders to resist the occupation of Palestine.

Concepts of gender and identity were analysed by women from Europe, Palestine and Israel at a conference organised by the *Centro di Documentazione delle Donne* in Bologna, Italy - *Many Women, One Planet* — in 1992, and informed the thinking of many Women in Black about transversal politics.

By the mid-1990s, Cynthia drew on their work and that of Nira Yuval-Davis, to develop and deepen this theory of transversal politics:

In 'transversal politics', perceived unity and homogeneity are replaced by dialogues, which give recognition to the specific positionings of those who participate in them as well as to the 'unfinished knowledge' that each such situated positioning can offer. (Yuval-Davis, 1997:130-1)

Cynthia took part in and studied three feminist anti-war projects for her book, *The Space Between Us — Negotiating Gender and National Identities in Conflict* (Cockburn 1998), with the explicit aim: 'to fill the container "transversal politics" with content'. (Cockburn, 1998:9).

Research into the work of the three organisations helped to further develop a theory of transversal politics in practice: The Women's Support Network — women's community centres working in Catholic and Protestant working-class Belfast, Northern Ireland; *Bat Shalom* — 'offspring of peace' — an alliance of Israeli Jewish and Palestinian women; and the Medica Women's Therapy Centre in Zenica, central Bosnia-Herzegovina, established in 1993 to respond to the needs of women and children traumatised by rape, bereavement and uprooting in the nationalist aggression involved in the break-up of Yugoslavia.

> Transversal politics answers to a need to conceptualise a democratic practice of a particular kind, a process that can on the one hand look for commonalities without being arrogantly universalist, and on the other affirm difference without being transfixed by it. Transversal politics is the practice of creatively crossing (and re-drawing) the borders that mark significant politicised differences. It means empathy without sameness, shifting without tearing up your roots. (Cynthia Cockburn and Lynette Hunter, *Soundings*, issue 12, 1999)

Cynthia further developed the theory of transversal politics in *The Line — Women, Partition, and the Gender Order in Cyprus* (Cockburn, 2004). *The Line* explores the work of a women's organisation — Hands Across the Divide — that reached across the partition line dividing Cyprus between Greek Cypriot South and Turkish Cypriot North. Cynthia was able to cross the line, while it was illegal for women on each side to cross over.

Women from both sides of the line met with Cynthia in London in 2002, after she had visited them in Cyprus, and agreed a constitution for Hands Across the Divide (HAD). The women then engaged Marie Mulholland, an experienced political activist who had been involved in getting women's interests taken into account in the peace process in Northern Ireland, to spend two weeks working with them.

By the time Marie left, the group had committed itself to working out a set of shared values and goals, as women, for the kind of changes they wanted peace to bring. (Cockburn, 2004:166)

Following intensive bi-communal negotiations under EU and UN auspices, the women heard the extraordinary announcement in April 2003 that the barrier between North and South Cyprus had been opened by the Turkish Republic of Northern Cyprus.

While they did not end partition, of course, and there were many difficulties remaining, the experience of those women working across borders developed and further honed WiB theories around transversal politics:

> Underlying transversal politics are several valuable insights (see for instance, Yuval-Davis 1997): First, standpoint epistemology, which recognizes that from each positioning the world is seen differently. There are many truths, and their reconciliation, or approximation, can be achieved only through dialogue. Second, respect for each other's realities and the perspectives they generate is essential and must include acknowledgement of the unequal power inherent in different positions. Third, what you are likely to want cannot be read from your positionality or 'name', and it's only on the basis of common values (not shared 'identity') that alliance for action becomes possible. (Cockburn, 2007:205)

Returning to Belgrade in 2004, Cynthia interviewed Staša Zajović, the coordinator of *Žene u Crnom* (Women in Black — *ŽuC*):

Staša explained that *ŽuC* did not think in terms of 'reconciliation', a notion that 'suggests we are different peoples who have to resolve a dispute'. On the contrary, they were all Yugoslavs who had been named and divided by nationalist politicians and militarists intent on erasing every indication of similarity and shared existence. It was not a question of 'reconciling' therefore, but of refusing the arbitrary barriers placed between people, re-establishing connection and seeking political grounds for solidarity. (Cockburn, 2007:103)

The interview was part of research into Cynthia's next book, *From Where We Stand — War, Women's Activism and Feminist Analysis* (Cockburn, 2007). *From Where We Stand* includes the voices of women on different sides of conflicts in the former Yugoslavia and Israel Palestine, working together for peace with justice, refusing racism, enmity and collective guilt. It describes transnational networks of women opposing US and Western European militarism and the so-called 'war on terror' and its accompanying racism.

The research took Cynthia 80,000 miles over two years, examining women's activism in wars as far apart as Sierra Leone, Colombia and India to answer the question:

Women who want to actively engage in opposition to militarism and war often choose to organise separately as women. Why ...? (Cockburn, 2007:1)

She concluded:

Antimilitarist and anti-war feminism is by definition multi-dimensional, taking as its scope not just 'body politics' but a far wider range of concerns. For a start, it cannot fail to have *a critique of capitalism*, and new forms of imperialism and colonization, class exploitation and the thrust for global markets, since these are visibly implicated among the causes and motors of militarism and war. Next, since many wars involve intra-state and inter-state nationalisms, this feminism also has that cluster *race/culture/religion/ethnicity* in view. In these two significant relational fields of class and race, this feminism perceives the working of gender relations and is alert to how they intersect …

This feminism defends international *human rights and women's rights,* negated in war, and the development of international justice. It has a sense of women's marginalization and *under-representation in political systems,* as we see from women activists' efforts at the UN. Clearly, then, this is a *holistic feminism* (Cockburn, 2007: 228).

Cynthia and many other feminist activists contributed to the development of a range of theories around holistic feminism, women's marginalisation and under-representation, and a gender analysis of the continuum of violence. In an article for openDemocracy 50.50 (Cockburn 25.11.2012) she developed the links between violence in war and male violence against women in peacetime:

When we're looking for the links between war violence and violence against women in peacetime, I think we need to look for causality, influence, flowing in both directions. Put briefly, violence in our everyday cultures, deeply gendered, predisposes societies to accept war as normal. And the violence of militarisation and war, profoundly gendered, spills back into everyday life and increases the quotient of violence in it.

This continuum was further developed in another article for openDemocracy 50.50 on 'World disarmament? Start by disarming masculinity' (Cockburn, 3.4.2015):

Over a span of twenty years I've had the privilege to meet and work with groups of feminist activists, in a dozen countries, many of them in the Global South. They are generating a more and more coherent narrative *about the causes of war. One of the things I've learned from them is that war doesn't stand alone. It›s helpful to see it as part of a continuum of violence.* That continuum persists along a scale of force (fist to bomb), a scale of time (peacetime, pre-war, wartime, post-war), a scale of place (bedroom, city, continent) and so on. As peace activists, they say, we have to look for the organisational, economic, social and psychological connections along the continuum and address it as a whole. One of the things they notice is that *gender is a thread running through the continua in every direction. Men and women, masculinity and femininity, in relation to each other, feature throughout the spectrum of violence.* (Cockburn, 30.4.2015)

Women in Black partner organisations like the Women's International League for Peace and Freedom (WILPF) also argue that violence has a disproportionate impact on women, and that women have been underrepresented in peace-making processes.

When weapons are present, women are at significantly greater risk of experiencing sexual violence. In homes where a gun is accessible, women are much more likely to be murdered by an intimate partner. Weapons are commonly used against women as a form of psychological violence, preventing them from accessing safety, education, healthcare, and economic opportunities.

The Women's International League for Peace and Freedom

WILPF was founded in 1915 when 1,200 women from 12 countries travelled to a Congress of Women in The Hague to call for an end to the First World War. WILPF's national sections cover every continent, with an International Secretariat based in Geneva, and a New York office focused on the work of the United Nations.

Since it was established, WILPF has brought together women from around the world to work for peace by non-violent means and promote political, economic and social justice for all. It uses the international legal and political framework to achieve fundamental change in the way states conceptualise and address issues of gender, militarism, peace and security. Its strength lies in its ability to link the local and the international levels, including being the first women's peace organisation to gain consultative status at the United Nations (UN).[2]

WILPF's feminist voices were instrumental in achieving UN Security Council Resolution (UNSCR) 1325 on women, peace and security, adopted on 31 October 2000. The resolution reaffirms the important role of women in the prevention and resolution of conflicts, peace negotiations, peace-building, peacekeeping, humanitarian response and in post-conflict reconstruction, and stresses the importance of their equal participation and full involvement in all efforts for the maintenance and promotion of peace and security. Resolution 1325 urges all actors to increase the participation of women and incorporate gender perspectives in all UN peace and security efforts. It also calls on all parties to conflict to take special measures to protect women and girls from gender-based violence, particularly rape and other forms of sexual abuse, in situations of armed conflict.

However, by 2015, when UN Women published their Global Study on UNSCR 1325, it was clear that its promise had not yet been achieved: 'The world has lost sight of some of the key demands of the women's movement while advocating for the adoption of resolution 1325: reducing military expenditures, controlling the availability of armaments, promoting non-violent forms of conflict resolution, and fostering a culture of peace.'[3]

WILPF is clear that women have a crucial role to play in building peace, and campaigns for women to be at the table in all peace negotiations:

> Women make up half of the world's population. Yet their voices are rarely listened to when it comes to peace and security issues. Far too often, women affected by conflict are excluded from the negotiating table, overlooked as experts, and denied visas to countries where multilateral discussions are held.
>
> When women participate — not just in a symbolic way, but in a true, meaningful way — things happen. Their input completes the picture of what is needed on the ground. According to UN Women, the chances of a peace agreement lasting at least 15 years increase by 35% if women are included in the process behind it.[4]

Rita Manchanda, a feminist writer and activist in South Asia, pointed out that 'women's perspectives come from the margin or "from below" and therefore may produce better insights into transforming inter-group relations which involve asymmetries of power' (Manchanda et al. *Women Making Peace: Strengthening Women's Role in Peace Processes*, 2002:7).

This does not suggest that women, any more than men, are 'natural born peace-makers'. But most women have a different experience of war from that of men. Most women fear rape. A feminist view sees masculinist cultures as especially prone to violence, so women tend to have a particular perspective on security and something unique to say about war.

Women in Black internationally have consistently opposed war, but have only comparatively recently, and through listening to voices from the global south, realised that we need to provide a response to conventional and often masculine definitions of peace and security beyond the mere absence of war or threat to a nation state, but as the absence of threat to the well-being of people in the world.

This gendered analysis builds on earlier feminist peace theories:

> For many peace activists, 'peace' means simply an absence of war; for nuclear disarmers it may mean specifically a world without nuclear weapons. But for us, since our basic definition of society is that it is both patriarchal and capitalist, peace means more than that: it means eradicating the causes of war and violence from our society. (Feminism and Non-violence Study Group, 1983:39)

Cynthia Enloe provided a gendered understanding of the basic themes of feminism, fundamentalism, nationalism and militarism:

> Paying serious attention to women can expose how much power it takes to maintain the international political system in its current form. (Enloe, 1989:3)

Later, Cynthia Cockburn wrote in *Antimilitarism — Political and Gender Dynamics of Peace Movements*, exploring international anti-war, anti-militarist peace movements in Japan, Korea, Spain, Uganda, the UK and campaigns against NATO:

> With every decade that passes, human violence, amplified by developments in media and weaponry, gains a longer reach, has more power to destroy our psyches, our relationships and our world. Our survival may depend on our ability to generate, quite soon, a worldwide epochal movement, one capable of displacing the prevailing idea that violence is normal and inevitable, and substituting a different paradigm: the idea that violence is a matter of choice. It would mean supposing that there is almost always a less violent alternative, a less violent thought, word, intention, policy, strategy and action; that we can choose a path that leads, step by step, towards a very much less violent society than the one we live in. For that idea to

become hegemonic, to become universal 'common sense', requires a huge and effective social movement. To obtain that sweep and scope, a lot of people must be paying careful attention to each other's thoughts and aspirations, exploring and exchanging methods and negotiating tactical and strategic alliances. (Cockburn, 2012:1)

Women in Black groups exist in many countries, and in widely different political situations. For some, especially those living through war, theories about the relationship between gender and militarism are the most vital. Other women, living in relative peacetime, choose combating male violence against individual women, and campaigning for the right to abortion, contraception and control over their own bodies, as the centre of their activism. The theories that connect Women in Black across the world, as a result, include the continuum of violence against women, and a causal relationship between gender and war.

Women have recently intervened internationally to argue that if peace is to be more than a mere cessation of hostilities, 'security' must be redefined to mean the satisfaction of human needs, including comprehensive safety for women. Women's peace movements, worldwide, are theorising that gender power relations are significant among the causes of war, and transformative change in how we 'live' gender can be a significant resource for peace. (Cockburn, 2013, Abstract)

This is part of a holistic and transformative theory of feminism and peace developed by Cynthia Cockburn, standing on the shoulders of many other theorists and activists. Underpinning this definition of security is the practice of transversal politics, crossing borders and partitions to negotiate the space between us and find ways to end conflicts.

Gerda Lerner argued in 1986 that:

The system of patriarchy is a historic construct; it has a beginning; it will have an end. Its time seems nearly to have run its course — it no longer services the needs of men or women and in its inextricable linkage to militarism, hierarchy and racism it threatens the very existence of life on earth. (Lerner, 1986:229)

Thank you to all the Women in Black across the world who contributed to making this book — and who continue to cross borders for peace with justice.

Sue Finch

NOTES

1   https://www.wilpf.org/wp-content/uploads/2021/05/English-IWD-for-Peace-and-Disarmament-Statement.pdf (accessed 15 June 2021)

2   https://www.wilpf.org/the-perks-of-having-consultative-status-with-the-un (accessed 17 June 2021)

3   Global Study on UNSCR 1325 (2015 p207) https://wps.unwomen.org/ (accessed 15 June 2021)

4   https://www.wilpf.org/include-women/ (accessed 14 June 2021)

CHAPTER I

SPRINGING TO LIFE: WOMEN IN BLACK IN ISRAEL PALESTINE

Women in Black began in Israel — in West Jerusalem — on the first Friday in January 1988. The call these women made, to the Israeli public and government, was an explicit and focused appeal to 'End the Occupation', to terminate the Israeli state's military control of adjacent territories populated by Palestinians. In this original context, then, Women in Black's message was not, as it would later become in many of its manifestations, a generalised call for peace and non-violence. Rather it addressed a conflictual relationship between two peoples: Israeli Jews and Palestinians. Their stressful history of cohabitation in the region is long and eventful. Since Women in Black has subsequently spread to many far distant parts of the world, where few of us may be expected to have detailed knowledge of this context, we'll begin with a brief retrospective sketch.

Israel Palestine: some historical background

The Jews of today originate in an ethnocultural group, the Judaians, of whose emergence in the lands between the River Jordan and the eastern shore of the Mediterranean Sea, sometimes known as 'historical Palestine', there is evidence from the middle of the second millennium BCE. They claimed descent from a patriarch named Abraham, developed a monotheistic belief in a god they called Yahweh, and created a religious code embodied in a holy book, the Torah. 'Historical Palestine' was subject over the centuries to a succession of empires (Assyrian,

Babylonian, Roman, Ottoman) and saw the emergence of rival monotheistic religions — notably Christianity (in the first century of the Common Era) and Islam (in the seventh century CE). The people known today as Palestinians are predominantly Muslim by faith, while around one-tenth are Christians of various denominations.[1] Christians and Muslims, like Jews, believed themselves to be descended from Abraham. Jerusalem, a city at the heart of historical Palestine, remains a holy centre for all Abrahamic religions.

In the course of three millennia, many Jewish people were expelled or migrated far and wide from their turbulent birthplace in the Middle East. Some travelled west and north, to East and Central Europe and then across the Atlantic, to become the diaspora Jewish population known as Ashkenazi Jews. Many others moved east or south, and some populated the coast of North Africa, settling among 'Arab' populations. According to location, some of these were named Sephardic, others Mizrahi Jews. Many Jews experienced discrimination and persecution in these diasporas. There arose, among other nationalisms of the late nineteenth century CE, a movement, termed Zionism, to recover a Jewish 'homeland' back in Judea, now known as Palestine. Between the First and Second World Wars, Palestine was administered under Mandate by the British government, which supported this aspiration for a Jewish 'homeland'. In 1917, the Foreign Secretary, Arthur Balfour, wrote to Lord Rothschild of the Zionist Federation that 'His Majesty's government view with favour the establishment in Palestine of a national home for the Jewish people, and will use their best endeavours to facilitate the achievement of this object'. Lord Balfour added, perhaps naively, that 'nothing shall be done which may prejudice the civil and religious rights of the existing non-Jewish communities in Palestine' (Balfour Declaration, Davis 1987:16). Under the Mandate, many Jews, from both the Ashkenazi and Mizrahi diasporas, immigrated with the intention of founding a state with the support of the World Zionist Federation and the

Jewish Agency. In the armed conflict that followed, Jews and Palestinians fought each other and the British.

The genocidal persecution of Jews in Nazi Germany in the 1930s and 1940s strengthened international support for the creation of a Jewish state in the aftermath of the Second World War (Laqueur 2003:40). In 1947, the British Mandate was due to end. The United Nations stepped in, adopting a Partition Plan for Palestine that designated a Jewish state on 57 per cent of the Mandate territory and a separate Arab state on the remaining 43 per cent. Jerusalem and some other sites deemed holy by both peoples were given a special status under international control (Davis 1987). The Jewish authorities accepted the UN plan, which was greatly in their favour since Jewish individual and corporate land holdings amounted to no more than seven per cent of the area at that time. Not surprisingly, the Arab authorities, who had been excluded from the negotiations, rejected it. Thus, when on 15 May 1948 the UN-sanctioned State of Israel, *Medinat Yisrael,* was unilaterally declared by the Jews, it was attacked by the armed forces of surrounding Arab countries. The Jews prevailed, however, and in the fighting shifted the boundaries of the Israeli state outwards to encompass 78 per cent of the Mandate area. Four-fifths of the Palestinian Arab villages therein were purposefully destroyed and the Palestinian residents driven out, an event Palestinians commemorate as their *nakba,* or catastrophe. An estimated 156,000 Palestinians remained, although displaced, within the State of Israel, constituting a disadvantaged minority in what the Declaration of Establishment termed specifically a 'Jewish state' (Davis 1987:13). But 700,000 Palestinians fled, some to far distant countries, others encamping or re-homing just outside the Green Line, as Israel's designated state border was termed. These events were described by Ilan Pappe as a deliberate campaign of 'ethnic cleansing' by Israel (Pappe 2006).

In 1967, when the Israeli state had been in existence for almost twenty years, the 'Six Day War' with Jordan, Egypt and

Syria ended with Israel establishing military control over the largely Palestinian-populated territories of the West Bank of the Jordan, the coastal Gaza Strip and Sinai Peninsula in the south, and the Golan Heights in the north (Davis 1987). This Occupation — let's give it the capital initial it so often carries — was military, tough and unremitting. It inflicted mental and physical suffering on the already-traumatised Palestinians who had found refuge in these territories twenty years before. The occupiers imposed frequent curfews, closures of schools and nurseries, arbitrary arrests and detention without trial, often involving torture.

The Occupation divided Israeli opinion from the start and would continue to do so. As Amos Oz would write, much later, 'It is a fact that hundreds of thousands of Israelis are convinced — intellectually and emotionally — that if Israel keeps hold of the Occupied Territories then it will cease to exist. Nothing less than that. While hundreds of thousands of other Israelis are convinced that if Israel pulls out it will cease to exist. Nothing less than that' (Oz 1994:48). Interestingly, it was among those tasked with implementing the Occupation that a movement against it began. In 1978 a group of several hundred Israeli soldiers and reservists got together to write an 'open letter' to the Prime Minister calling for the Israeli government to persist in peace talks. They formed an organisation they called *Shalom Achshav*: Peace Now. It was neither strongly pacifist, nor particularly pro-Palestinian. It did, however, consistently voice opposition to the Occupation. Its mass demonstrations brought together those on the left and in the liberal centre, even religious people, who sought to avert annexation of the Occupied Territories, and achieve self-determination and statehood for Palestinians (Oz 1994:80).

Where were the women?

As an organisation, Peace Now appears to have been male-dominated and masculinist. Women, when present at all, played support roles. They were 'the envelope-stuffers and stamp-lickers', as Women in Black activist Hannah Safran later expressed it (Safran 2005:193). So where were women in Israeli peace politics? Indeed, where were women in Israeli society?

The Proclamation of Independence in 1948 had stated that Israel would maintain complete social and political equality for all its citizens, regardless of religion, race or sex. For all this, 'leadership, influence and dominance in virtually every area remained, indeed remains to this day, firmly in the hands of men' (Golan 1995:13). For one thing, the powerful Jewish religious establishment was a force sustaining the traditional gender division of roles in the Israeli state; as Galia Golan (a leading Israeli peace activist who co-founded Peace Now) put it, 'they succeeded in blackmailing virtually every governing coalition in the country to maintain religious control over vital aspects of citizens' rights' (ibid:14). Labor Zionism, the dominant political philosophy of the period, promoted the ideal of the Jewish *sabra*, the combative manly man. This masculinist ideal was served very well by the continuing militarisation of Israeli society. Every Jewish citizen was, had been or would be a soldier or a soldier's partner, parent or child. Although Jewish women too were required to perform military service, and increasingly in combat roles, the army somehow remained, for all that, a patriarchal institution. The Occupation redoubled the emphasis on militarism, and thus made yet more visible, in Simona Sharoni's words (a feminist scholar, activist and Professor of Women's and Gender studies in the US), 'the connections between, on the one hand, the social construction of gender identities and gender relations in Israel, and, on the other, the use of violence in the Occupied Territories and on the Israeli home front' (Sharoni 1994:122).

A women's movement seeking gender equality had gathered momentum in Israel, as it did in Western Europe and the USA, during the 1970s. In the early years, however, the movement comprised mainly Ashkenazi middle-class women, and stressed equality of culture and class as much as of sex-gender. In the 1973 elections, a Citizens Rights Movement led by Knesset member Shulamit Aloni won three seats in the Knesset: one of those elected was Marcia Freedman, an active feminist. She in turn led a movement for a Women's Party to compete in the ensuing elections in 1977. The Women's Party message was distinctive and fresh. Most notably, it made a clear connection between its goals of women's liberation and Palestinian freedom. 'We see Arab women ...', they wrote 'as sisters in a joint struggle for equal rights and equal opportunities, and we wait for the day when we will be able to shake hands across national boundaries' (Sharoni 1994:105).

But, despite a growing feminist movement, women's peace activism was slow to take hold in Israel. There was a particular impediment — as Yvonne Deutsch points out (Deutsch 1994). Women held deeply contradictory feelings about the Israeli military. As pacifists they might necessarily be unenthusiastic about how militarisation shaped the character and behaviour of Israeli Jewish men. One thing they had discovered was that 'a soldier who serves in the West Bank and Gaza Strip and learns that it is permissible to use violence against other people is likely to bring that violence back with him, upon his return to his community' (Sharoni 1995:120).

Yet given the enmity of the surrounding Arab nations, to be well armed seemed essential to Israel's survival. This ambivalence obscured women's perception of their husbands and sons as oppressors. An exceptional moment was when Israel invaded Lebanon in 1982. On this occasion many women were incensed to see their sons packed off to fight a war that, this time, the Israeli state had initiated. They organised in opposition to it.[2]

By 1987, the year before Women in Black's start-up, the Occupation had lasted for twenty years. On 9 December that year, an Israeli Defence Forces' truck in the Gaza Strip collided with a civilian car, killing four Palestinians. Nothing remarkable you might think. But this car crash was the spark that fired a Palestinian uprising against the Israeli state. Termed in Arabic the *intifada*, a word that implies 'rising up' and 'shaking off', it was an upsurge of impatience with the Occupation among the oppressed population of the West Bank and Gaza.

Outside the Green Line demarcating the Israeli state, there was an increasingly organised Palestinian political entity. The population had become more vocal, drawing the attention of the world to its pursuit of justice. In 1974, Yasser Arafat, Chairman of the Palestine Liberation Organisation (PLO), had already won recognition of Palestinians' right to independent statehood from more than half the United Nation's member states. Israel, however, remained intransigent. When Palestinian patience ran out on that fateful December day in 1987, their insurgency involved boycotts of the Israeli civil administration, strikes against Jewish employers and the widespread deployment against the Israeli Defence Forces of the minimal weapons available to them — stones, slingshots, Molotov cocktails. Israeli state forces hit back hard. During the six years of that *intifada*, 1,083 Palestinians were killed, of whom 282 were under the age of sixteen (Orr 1994:168).

During the *intifada,* violence by Israeli men against Israeli women, in the home and on the street, increased markedly. This was another prompt to political awareness among Israeli women. It made starkly clear how 'the violent patterns of behaviour that are used by the Israeli army against Palestinians in the West Bank and Gaza strip are part of a culture of unchallenged sexism, violence and oppression which women face daily on Israeli streets and in their homes' (Sharoni 1994:126).

This sense of sisterhood caused a small number of peace-minded women in Israel to get involved in support work among women in the Occupied Territories. They formed organisations to aid the growing number of Palestinian women political prisoners and families of deportees. And the suffering they saw being inflicted on Palestinians made them increasingly alert to their own sexual subordination. It is not surprising, then, that women were now inspired to action simultaneously on the issue of the Occupation *and* as feminists — as in the case of the Jerusalem women who started Women in Black.

Women in Black: the first step

This is how it came about. One group that sprang into existence that last week of December 1987 was called *Dai la Kibush* (End the Occupation). *Dai la Kibush* called for the Israeli government to negotiate with the representatives of the Palestine Liberation Organisation, for the purpose of creating an independent Palestinian state alongside Israel. Its branch in West Jerusalem began holding a weekly Friday demonstration — chosen as the beginning of Jewish Sha'bat and the day of Islamic congregational prayer. Gila Svirsky, a resident of Jerusalem, was one of the women who were not only close to the action but involved in it from the start (Svirsky 1996: Ch.1).[3] At that first *Dai la Kibush* demonstration, on the last Friday in December 1987, the organisers proposed that, to heighten the drama, the men should come dressed in white and the women in black. As it happened, while the women did don black, the men couldn't bring themselves to dress in white for the occasion and showed up in their usual garb. Gila continues,

> The women, though, looked dramatic — like a classical Greek chorus. To take advantage of the funereal effect, it was decided that the women would stand separately from the men. A little more interest was, indeed, generated among spectators, which encouraged the group to try again the next week, this time at the Jerusalem Cinematheque, only women, wearing black (Svirsky 1996: Ch.1).

Gila goes on to describe how the following week, on 2 January 1988, the first truly 'Women in Black' vigil was held — that is to say, the first that intentionally comprised women alone, eight of them, dressed in black. A few supportive men remained nearby to distribute leaflets to onlookers. Two of the women, Ruth Cohen and Ida Bilu, had prepared large black signs in the shape of hands, with the Hebrew words *Dai LaKibush* in bold white lettering. One of the women who attended that vigil was Raya Rotem. A war widow herself, she was particularly keen on the idea of the women wearing black. She now called on a wider circle of women to attend the demonstration of the following week. Thus, on 9 January, as Gila puts it, 'the women made the plunge from anonymity into mob recognition'. The vigil site was in the heart of downtown Jerusalem, on the busy corner of Jaffa Road and Ben Yehuda Street. Around fifteen women attended this time (Svirsky 1996: Ch.1).[4] The signs were now in three languages: Hebrew, Arabic and English. Ruth Cohen displayed a big drawing she had made of an Israeli soldier violently clubbing a Palestinian. This time the vigil drew a heavy reaction from passers-by. The location exposed them to public fury. Hagar Roublev, one of the key organisers of the Jerusalem group, recalled later, 'I came home covered with spit'.[5] A decision was made to move the weekly vigil to Paris Square, where they were still visible to many drivers and pedestrians, but were able to stand raised above the pavement, on a low wall, a little distanced from harm. So, writes Gila,

> Although the vigil was held weekly as a woman's action and developed its own momentum, the *Dai LaKibush* organization continued to regard it as one of its activities. It was not easy for them to relinquish parental control and ownership of their all-woman spinoff. At an organizing meeting held several months into the vigil, one of the leaders of *Dai LaKibush* announced that a number of decisions would have to be made about the Women in Black vigil. 'You're relieved of all decisions about Women in Black,' the founding mothers told him, 'We don't belong to you anymore.' Thus, Women in Black was launched as an independent, all-woman enterprise. (Svirsky 1996: Ch.1)

The idea of a women-only, black-clad, silent vigil spread from Jerusalem, first to the cities of Haifa and Tel Aviv. The women in Haifa began to hold vigils on International Women's Day, 8 March 1988. They initiated a telegram campaign to address their messages to the Israeli government and military. The women in Tel Aviv, for their part, took a screen into the street and projected images illustrating the oppression occurring in the Occupied Territories. After a few weeks of this, their action too morphed into a Women in Black vigil. Their messages were bold, including the call for 'peace negotiations with the PLO'. The vigils in these two cities included women experienced in feminist projects such as rape crisis work and Haifa's noted women's centre, Isha l'Isha (the oldest feminist grassroots organisation in Israel). The activists in these projects became something of a vanguard element in Women in Black in Israel. Their vigils attracted a good deal of abuse from passers-by. Often the insults were expressed in strongly sexualised terms. 'Whores of Arafat', passing drivers yelled. People threw eggs, fruit, water at the women. They were often harassed by street gangs of young anti-Palestinian men.

Now WiB vigils began to spread to other Israeli towns such as Kfar Sava, Beer Sheva, Acre and Rehovot. Women of several kibbutzim came out too. First was Kibbutz Nahson, soon followed by Kibbutz Gan Shmuel, and, in the south, Samar. These were especially important as most kibbutzim had originated with socialist ideals of equality for all. One feisty vigil led by women of Kibbutz Megiddo and including participants from other kibbutzim and moshavim,[6] some quite far distant, and from the towns of Nazareth and Afula, provocatively positioned themselves at a busy road junction in the Wadi Ara, an area of mixed Jewish and Arab residence, adjacent to a prison where many Palestinians were incarcerated. Notably, some Palestinians from the Occupied Territories, including some men, came to join the Megiddo vigils. The placards were in Hebrew, Arabic and English.[7]

However, not all the male kibbutz members were supportive of the vigils. Some were highly critical, and would confront
the women, shouting abuse as at the Jerusalem vigil: 'you are
traitors', 'death to Arabs', and so on. Gila Svirsky recounts
how a group of WiB approached an ideological coordinator
of the kibbutz movement to ask for his support for the vigils.
He responded by demanding the women sign a statement that
included a Zionist perspective on the conflict. They refused,
and six women met with him. Three hours later, he was so well
persuaded of their case that he issued a letter to all kibbutzim
encouraging women to join Women in Black vigils. This
prompted new vigils and drew more women into the existing
ones (Svirsky 1996: Ch. 5).

The number of vigils grew steadily. The WiB process
and style was, after all, easy to emulate. The principles were
somehow informally but swiftly agreed and passed on. First
and foremost, there was the wearing of black. This symbolised
mourning and it counteracted any tendency to present
women as 'sexual', 'feminine' or 'pretty' — no pink here!
White garments, which had been chosen by some women's
groups demonstrating against the Lebanon war of 1982, were
rejected this time. Black spoke of sorrow and seemed more
appropriate. Besides, since most women had something black
in their wardrobes, it was a cheap and easy option. Secondly,
there was the maintaining of silence. This was adopted as a
principle — the women wished to allow their bodily presence
to speak silently for them. In practice, however, many found
it hard to remain silent. Third, there was the regularity of the
hour, usually from 1 — 2 p.m., and the day, Friday. Fourth,
there was the consistency of place: a prominent street side or
crossroads position visible to both pedestrians and car drivers.
There was agreement that each vigil would be autonomous, but
that within the vigil, the decision-making would be consen-
sual, including choice of message. There was, however, little
variation in signage, most vigils sticking simply to 'End the

Occupation'. It was agreed that each woman would contribute one shekel per week to cover common expenses. By December 1988, almost a year after the first WiB vigil, Gila Svirsky estimates there were around 500 Women in Black standing weekly in 23 vigils. A year later, in December 1989, there were 120 women in the Jerusalem vigil alone, and an estimated 39 vigils country wide. Six hundred women travelled to Jerusalem to celebrate that anniversary.

In addition to vigils, the women organised or participated in a number of sizeable events. As early as January 1988 a group emerged, with many participants, to organise the making of a 'Peace Quilt' containing hundreds of panels embroidered with women's peace messages, imagined as a symbolic cover for a future negotiating table. The outcome was a colourful quilt more than 100 metres long. That June, a date that marked the twenty-first anniversary of the start of the Occupation, 400 Israeli Jewish and Israeli Palestinian women marched and demonstrated, carrying the quilt around the Knesset building, the seat of the Israeli Parliament (Safran 2005: 191-202). Some months later, on the first anniversary of the start of the *intifada,* women mounted a conference entitled 'Occupation or Peace: A Feminist Perspective'. It was attended by several hundred Israeli Jewish women, and Palestinian women from both Israel and the Occupied Territories. Simona Sharoni was there. Later, she wrote, 'All the speakers made explicit connections between women's struggles for liberation and equality and the Palestinian struggles for national liberation and self-determination. Another set of connections made explicit was that between the violence of war and occupation and violence against women' (Sharoni 1995:117). Then, in May 1989, around fifty women from Israel and the Occupied Territories, including representatives of the Palestine Liberation Organisation, attended an international conference held in Brussels: 'Give Peace a Chance: Women Speak Out'. A few months later, on 9 September 1989, Women in Black organised a national conference at Kibbutz Harel in central Israel, attended by 300 women (Svirsky 1996: Ch. 6).

A good deal of activity occurred around the end of 1989 and the start of 1990, as Women in Black turned two years old. On Friday 29 December 1989, a women's peace conference was held, jointly organised by Jewish and Palestinian women, and attended by women from Italy, other European countries and North America. It was mounted in the context of an international initiative termed '1990 Time For Peace', and ended with demands on the Israeli government for a negotiated peace with the PLO and the creation of an independent Palestinian state. The vigil in Jerusalem that day attracted an estimated 2,000 women. It was followed by a march through Jerusalem, from Paris Square in the West across to East (Arab) Jerusalem, where it was joined by several thousand women from the Palestinian territories, likewise dressed in black. Even this event was surpassed, however, the following day, when a demonstration, Hands Around Jerusalem, brought a human chain of 30,000 women and men to encircle the Old City of Jerusalem, expressing the desire for Jews and Palestinians to live in friendship side by side. WiB was fully part of this mass event, alongside Peace Now and other Israeli peace groups. Gila reports that it was met by 'an onslaught of police brutality — billy clubs, water cannons, tear gas and rifles' (Svirsky 1996: Ch. 6).[8]

Who were the Women in Black?

We should now look more closely at the vigils and ask who, exactly, were the Women in Black there? Gila Svirsky calculated that 84 per cent were highly educated (mostly in the humanities, many with higher degrees). No less than 85 per cent were in income-producing work, compared with only 48 per cent of women in Israel at that time. Most, however, were in low-paying 'women's work', employed as teachers, librarians or care workers in kibbutzim. They were predominantly Ashkenazi (thus 'white' and mainly middle class) Jews. Fully 87 per cent were not religious. More than half were living without a partner and a quarter had no children. Gila points out that these latter are very high proportions 'in a country addicted to marriage and children'. As to age, the span was very wide, from teenagers to women in their nineties, with an average of 47 years (Svirsky 1996: Ch.7). A separate study by Hanna Safran reckoned that 30 per cent of WiB vigillers were lesbians (Safran 2005:200).[9]

Politically, WiB was a mix of more or less leftist/socialist women. It was also a mix of Zionist and anti-Zionist women. Most vigils did not fly the Israeli flag, but some chose to do so. Some vigils sought an end to the Occupation by means of a 'two-state solution', with a Palestinian state sitting alongside a Jewish one. Others — such as members of the leftist *Nitzotz* group — wished to see a shared multi-ethnic state comprising Israel and the Occupied Territories (Svirsky 1996: Ch. 7). Despite such differences between vigils, and among the individuals in any one of them, WiB managed to agree, informally, on certain principles. All were agreed, for instance, that they should not respond to the abuse thrown at them, tangle with the young men who attacked them, or in any way provoke the police. Indeed, they sometimes proactively contacted the police, seeking their protection. They were also committed to highlighting the historic oppression of Jews as well as the wrongs done to Palestinians. Thus, the Jerusalem vigil group hammered out an agreed statement that read,

> We, Women in Black, citizens of Israel, have held our weekly protest vigil since the beginning of the Intifada. This vigil has grown out of Israeli society and expresses our need to actively and strongly oppose the occupation. The black clothing symbolizes the tragedy of both peoples, the Israeli and the Palestinian. (Svirsky 1996: Ch. 7)

Not all vigillers were in full agreement with the way the Women in Black movement proceeded. Erella Shadmi, for example, an Israeli Jewish researcher and writer, is one vigiller who was somewhat critical of WiB as it developed in Israel. She stood with the Jerusalem vigil from 1990 to 1995. It was, she admits, very different, in its silence, its black dress and repetitive weekly occurrence at a constant time and place, from anything else going on in Israel at the time. But she notes several weaknesses. For one thing, despite WiB's apparent commitment to structurelessness and inclusion, it tended, she felt, to be hierarchical and to use unnecessarily 'lofty language'. In practice, only a small proportion of the women vigillers took the decisions. Naomi Chazan adds to this analysis: 'Lower income women and residents of development towns and the poorer neighbourhoods of the major cities are distinctly under-represented, indicating a close link between personal background and peace activism' (Chazan 1993:157). This is not unconnected with a criticism Shadmi goes on to make: WiB was incapable of attracting and holding more than a very few Mizrahi women, who felt alienated and some-how 'unfit for WiB'. Mizrahi or Eastern Jews are descended from Jewish communities that existed in the Middle East, North Africa and Asia, and are seen as having lower status in Israel. Shadmi pointed out that the dominance of Ashkenazi and absence of Mizrahi women contradicted WiB's apparent aim of challenging the existing order (Shadmi, 2000, 2004). Secondly, WiB fell short, she felt, on the feminist front. The movement declined in part because they refused to expand their strategy and to enlarge their political statement beyond the slogan 'Stop the Occupation' or to incorporate any clear feminist or other message into their protest. In fact, they refused to capitalize on their own achievements. Consequently, the feminist practice they developed remained confined to the vigils and did not become an integral part of Israeli politics in general. (Shadmi 2000:31)

Although, Shadmi admitted, WiB was a 'unique and van-guard action' and 'a vital and passionate social discourse with the street', ultimately, she felt, the political practice the women developed remained their own, enclosed within the group itself, incapable of being incorporated into politics. Consequently, its transformative power ... was neutralized and circumscribed, and the women remained on the margins of politics. (ibid.31)

We shall have reason to think back on these limitations in Israeli WiB as we read in later chapters of the difficulties women faced in other countries. Nonetheless, we must remember that others saw Israeli WiB in a more positive light, as 'a unique phenomenon in the history and politics of Israeli society', to quote Israeli Jewish WiB Hanna Safran (Safran 2005:192). One measure of its significance is the working partnership the vigil groups established with several other women's peace initiatives during 1988, resulting in the creation, that November, of an enduring umbrella body, the Women and Peace Coalition, in which WiB would go on to play a leading role. An early member of the Coalition was TANDI, the Movement of Democratic Women in Israel, the women's branch of the Israeli Communist Party. The Peace Quilt group, mentioned above, was involved in the Coalition. So was the feminist magazine *Noga*, along with Neled, Machsom Watch and New Profile, a movement supporting those refusing state military service (ibid.). From May 1988, first in Tel Aviv and later in Jerusalem, a group named Women for Women Political Prisoners (WFWPP) was formed, to provide practical and legal help to Palestinian women in the Occupied Territories incarcerated by the occupying Israel forces; this group too joined the Coalition (Deutsch 1994). The Women's International League for Peace and Freedom (WILPF), which had a branch in Israel, likewise signed up. An initiative similar in spirit to Women in Black, but initially separate from it, was *Bat Shalom*, in which Jewish Israeli women linked up with Palestinian women of the Jerusalem Center for Women. It grew out of a dialogue of Palestinian and Israeli women begun in 1989 in Brussels under the title 'Women Speak Out for Peace' (Golan 1995).

Women of the Jerusalem WiB group, which included some women from *Bat Shalom* and the Jerusalem Center, together with WFWPP, subsequently founded *Shani* (Israeli Women's Alliance to End the Occupation), which comprised both Jewish and Palestinian women and conducted study groups for political education and to discuss solutions to the Occupation. *Shani* joined the Coalition. So, too, in 1989, did *Reshet*, the Israeli Women's Peace Net, formed that year by women of the political centre and academics. The Women and Peace Coalition organised several conferences. The evolution of these partner organisations that gathered in the Women and Peace Coalition may be seen as carrying the political message of the movement beyond the limitations imposed by the narrower consensus of Women in Black itself.

Jewish and Palestinian women: reaching across difference

Oddly, one highly significant feature of the women who came together to mount Women in Black vigils was not mentioned in the analyses of the membership by Gila Svirsky and Hannah Safran, referred to above. There were both Jewish and Palestinian Israeli women among the vigillers. Strangely, neither author states their relative numbers. Yet it will be clear that WiB activism in Israel Palestine involved a careful partnership between women of these two distinct ethno-cultural groups. In this it differed from the WiB experience as it unfolded in most other countries. The story is made more complex by a duality in the relationship between Jewish women and Palestinian women. On the one hand, vigils drew their activists from an Israeli population comprising both Jews and Palestinians. Thus Women in Black itself was mixed on this ethno-cultural dimension. And on the other hand, these Jewish and Palestinian Israeli WiB were together reaching out with their message of peace to the Palestinian community on the other side of the Israeli state border: those subject to Occupation by the Israeli state.

Let's consider the Israeli Palestinian women first. Their partnership with Jewish sisters was one that had to be created and sustained across a significant degree of inequality. To bring them clearly into view, David Grossman, an Israeli Jew, native of Jerusalem, reports in his book, *Sleeping on a Wire*, on interviews he carried out among Israeli Palestinians in 1991 (Grossman 1993:180). He tells us how, for the preceding forty years, these Palestinian 'remainers' in the newly-created State of Israel — around one-fifth of the population at the start — had lived quietly subordinated to the Jewish majority. They were governed under military law until 1966. In the centre and south of the country, they lived in districts in which they were the minority, though in the northern districts of Galilee and the Wadi Ara they constituted as much as three-quarters of the population. Around half of them were technically 'present absentees', cast out of their original homes and land. While Israel's Law of Return guaranteed citizenship to any and every individual in the world who could claim one Jewish grandparent, Israel's Arabs had no right of return even to their own former properties. They brought up their families and maintained their cultural lives as best they could, labouring for Jewish employers, creating small enterprises and farming what smallholdings they could access.

Although Israel's constitutive document, its Declaration of Independence, in principle gives equal rights to these Arab citizens, in practice there was and is considerable discrimination. As Grossman points out, they have been largely excluded from political power and influence, holding less than 2 per cent of senior positions in government ministries and associated bodies. The Israeli state had never required, nor had it permitted, Palestinian citizens to serve in the armed forces at that time, although Palestinian Israelis can now volunteer for the Israeli Defence Force. Given the high value placed on the military and military service in Israel, this was not the privilege it might seem, but on the contrary damaging discrimination. Israeli Palestinians, Grossman concludes, 'are half citizens and the state, for them, is half democratic. They are in the middle —

between citizenship and subjection' (Grossman 1993:181). Their disadvantage has had an economic dimension too. For instance, Israel controls all major water resources, and distributed more than four times as much water to Israeli settlers on Palestinian land than to Palestinian farmers themselves. Drawing on statistics for 1989, Grossman estimated that 92 per cent of Israeli Palestinian wage-earners that year were on the bottom half of the social scale. Half were living below the poverty line. Six times as many Palestinian as Jewish children were living in poverty (Grossman 1993:110). Eighteen years later, in 2006-7, Israeli Palestinian organisations would publish a series of papers that became known as the 'Vision Documents'. These were proud and defiant assertions of Palestinian rights and called for historical redress, equity and power-sharing in the Israeli state. They were angrily denounced by Israeli Jewish politicians and media. Nothing had changed (Peleg and Waxman 2011), and little has changed since.

Grossman found many of the Israeli Palestinian individuals he interviewed in the early 1990s to be on the defensive, because they were hearing criticism from Palestinians they believed must be more 'genuine' than themselves — that is, those who had left Israel when the state formed. 'You stayed on to serve the enemy, like a woman who, raped by a man, agrees to be his mistress,' they heard them say (Grossman 1993:39). One of the Palestinian remainers told him, 'I'm caught in the perfect paradox — I have to be a loyal citizen of a country that declares itself not to be my country but rather the country of the Jewish people' (ibid.16). When the *intifada* began, the Israeli Palestinians felt challenged to clarify their feelings and their loyalties. 'Are we part of it or not part of it?' they wondered. (ibid.15)

A different difference: Palestinian women and the intifada

But how did the Israeli women of Women in Black, Jewish and Palestinian both, relate to the Palestinian women living in the

Occupied Territories, for whose liberation from occupation the Women in Black vigils cried out? In 1973, Palestinian women in the Territories had founded a body, the Palestinian Union of Women's Work Committees (PUWWC), to bring women's organisations together into a more effective force. The political aim of the PUWWC was two-fold: national freedom and women's liberation. Its activist women contributed to the national struggle for the overthrow of the Israeli Occupation, and statehood for Palestinians. But they also addressed women's oppression in an underdeveloped socio-economic structure and in the context of patriarchal religions that positioned women as the appendage of men, to serve the husband in the house and rear the children. The PUWWC were particularly effective in organising women working solely in the home. While 'house-wives' (for want of a better word) were 55 per cent of Palestinian women in the Occupied Territories, they were 73 per cent of the membership of PUWWC. (VLD 1988)

These women were deeply affected by the *intifada* of 1987. And, strangely, despite their increased oppression and suffering, they were in some ways strengthened thereby. Due to many Palestinian men being absent from the home — participating in the uprising, imprisoned, disappeared or in exile — more women were obliged to go out and earn an independent living to support their children, gaining knowledge, skills and confidence as a result.

Seeing Palestinian women so fully engaged in the uprising inspired many more Israeli Palestinian women to self-awareness and activism. Nabila Espanioli, an Israeli Palestinian born in Nazareth, described how it awoke in them both a feminist consciousness and what she called a 're-palestinianization', resulting in a greater willingness to demand rights both as women and as Palestinians (Espanioli 1994:112). Nazareth is in the north of Israel. Here, from the start, the WiB vigillers were Israeli Palestinian women. Nabila, writing as one of them, compared the vigil in Nazareth with that in the Jewish cities of Haifa and Tel Aviv.

> In Nazareth, we Women in Black … ask ourselves
> the same questions, but also others: how to find new
> ways of expressing our solidarity with the struggle of
> Palestinians in the occupied territories, how to persuade
> the government of Israel to negotiate with the Palestine
> Liberation Organization, how to help our brothers and
> sisters in the occupied territories, how to involve more
> women in our activities, and how to develop actions in
> keeping with our culture that would have an impact on
> the Arab street. (ibid.)

The *intifada* also brought to some Israeli Jewish women,
though far from all, a greater awareness of Palestinian realities:
what the Palestinian population of the Occupied Territories
had been suffering. Many Israeli Jewish women, perhaps the
majority, had little contact in the normal run of things with
Palestinian women — even those living beside them within
the Israeli state. Gila Svirsky was candid in explaining how
ignorant she now understands herself to have been, before
her experience in Women in Black, of Palestinians and their
different realities. She described her learning curve this way:

> When I first stood on the Jerusalem vigil, the third
> week of that vigil in January 1988, I brought a sign that
> said something like 'Stop the Violence on Both Sides'.
> Astonishing, isn't it, the lack of political acumen that
> suggests? A couple of months into the vigil, Judy Blanc,
> one of the radicals, invited me to her home for dinner,
> where Rita Giaccomon, a Palestinian feminist from Bir
> Zeit University [in the West Bank] was also invited. I
> had never before personally met a Palestinian. I was
> 42 years old and living in Israel since the age of 19!
> Rita told me things about life under Occupation that I
> found hard to believe. Soon after, I made my first visit
> to a Palestinian home in the Territories, and all this
> began my education.[10]

Gila added that she believed her learning trajectory was no different from that of many WiB vigillers. However, a small minority of Jewish Israeli women had long been alert to the particular plight of their Palestinian sisters under occupation in the Territories, due both to their positioning as women in relation to Palestinian men, and their harassment by the Israeli Defence Forces. Come the *intifada*, they now saw those women participating to the full in the uprising. Ebba Augustin was in the Occupied Territories conducting research in 1987 when the uprising[11] began. She wrote,

> Witnessing the *Intifada* shaping the life of people, I was amazed by the sudden power of women. Women of all ages were at the forefront of the demonstrations, they organized food, clothes and equipment for their besieged communities, with never-tiring effort they queued for papers, for stamps, for visits to their arrested menfolk and children. Women showed an amazing ability to sustain the spirit of survival in their families during days and weeks of curfew, under gas attack and siege ... (Augustin 1993)

The *intifada* thus made Jewish women, from their side of the relationship, more acutely aware of the value and importance of their activist partnership with Palestinian women, on whichever side of the Green Line they lived. Lily Traubman and Yehudit Zeidenberg, for instance, writing of the vigils they organised in the Wadi Ara, said

> The participation of Palestinians was of supreme importance, increasing and deepening the significance of the demonstration, helping us to develop new understandings of the conflict. It radicalized us and with time we created other activities, no longer solely about the Occupation but also about the civil and political inequalities inside Israel.[12]

Israeli WiB's decline and change: the Gulf War and Oslo Accords

The Gulf War of 1990-91 was challenging for Women in Black. Iraqi forces, under the leadership of Saddam Hussein, occupied Kuwait in August 1990, and some months later, in January 1991, the combined forces of the USA, the UK, Saudi Arabia and Egypt, amongst others, launched a five-week aerial and naval bombardment, followed by a ground assault, to expel them. Yasser Arafat and the PLO voiced support for Saddam Hussein. Israel, on the contrary, was part of the Western alliance, and, in response, Iraq fired Scud missiles on civilian targets in Israel.

When the war broke out, many WiB groups around the country paused their vigils. The Jerusalem vigillers were ordered by the police to halt theirs. But the women held a meeting to discuss their response. They were divided. Many of them felt that the war was entirely wrong, and they should protest against it. Others supported American involvement, feeling that the USA was fighting the war on behalf of Israel (Svirsky 1996: Ch. 7). Jewish and Palestinian women found themselves on opposite sides in this conflict, and this greatly challenged the WiB alliance between them. The Women and Peace Coalition did organise a demonstration against the war, but many vigils ceased at this point. Although WiB in Jerusalem, Haifa and Tel Aviv subsequently led a modest return to the practice of vigils, they never really recovered. Ironically, WiB was awarded the Aachen Peace Prize in September 1991. The Jerusalem group organised a conference to discuss how to revive the movement. But by the end of the year WiB was virtually dead in Israel. Only a handful of vigils struggled on (Deutsch 1994).[13]

What little of WiB that remained was further challenged by the peace process that subsequently began between Israel and the Palestine Liberation Organisation (PLO). It was announced on 29 August 1993 that representatives of the Israeli government had been secretly meeting with representatives of the PLO in Oslo, Norway. The Jerusalem women responded with a vigil saying 'Yes to Peace'. At last they could use such words! (Svirsky 1996: Ch.7) On 13 September, photos of Yasser Arafat and President Yitshak Rabin signing a Declaration of Principles, and shaking hands on the White House lawn, were broadcast across the globe. It was almost six years since the start of the *intifada* — and of WiB. The Oslo Accords, as they were known, looked like ending the Occupation. We know better now, of course. But on 20 October, Jerusalem WiB voted to end their vigil. Most of the few remaining vigils in Israel followed suit. Hannah Safran records that the following year, in October 1994, there were only two vigils left in Israel and in 1996 WiB was dismantled entirely. It seemed Women in Black in Israel was dead (Safran 2005). There was indeed a pause. But it was not in fact the end of Israeli WiB. In December 2000, when a second *intifada* broke out, WiB came back to life and regular vigils resumed in Israel.

In 2021, London WiB Pat Gaffney commented:

> I have been fortunate to link up with Women in Black Jerusalem on two of my most recent visits to the country. Searching them out and standing with them is an important act of solidarity for me. First, because making connections with peacemakers in Israel is essential and not always easy. Secondly, because it helps me understand the culture of militarism and occupation that they are working against.

In the meantime, however, let us move on to see how WiB spread to other countries — first, across the Atlantic.

NOTES

1   There are also sizeable minorities of Druze and Bedouin. See Peleg and Waxman 2011.

2   This explains why some in the ensuing women's peace activism identified specifically as 'mothers'. Other women however found it distasteful to use 'motherhood' as a political platform and chose instead a radical feminist expression of resistance.

3   In 1996, Gila Svirsky, a key activist in Women in Black from its earliest years, wrote a detailed and fascinating account of the movement, titled Standing for Peace: A History of Women in Black in Israel. It is currently retrievable from the website <http://www.gilasvirsky.com/wib_book.html> (accessed 14.6.2021). Since page numbers are not referable, we have cited chapter numbers when quoting from this account.

4   They were Dafna Amit, Mimi Ash, Judy Blanc, Ruth Cohen, Yvonne Deutsch, Ruth Elraz, Hava Halevi, Dafna Kaminer, Lily Moed, Tikva Honig Parnass, Maya Rosenfeld, Raya Rotem, Hagar Roublev, Hagit Segal and Hagit Shlonsk.

5   Hagar Roublev was one of the founders, leaders and central personalities of Israeli Women in Black. She gave rise to a certain amount of controversy. This is how Gila Svirsky depicted Hagar in her account (mentioned in Endnote iii above). 'One of the founders, Hagar, took upon herself the role of "master sergeant", enforcing discipline of all sorts. She would make a round of the group several times during the vigil and let us hear her rebukes: "Stop talking, this isn't a tea party"; "Tell your boyfriend to stand behind you, he's blocking the view of you"; "Buy yourself a pure black shirt that doesn't have that design in the corner — or wear it inside out"; and the perennial "You're late!". Many, probably most of us, were intimidated by Hagar, with her strong presence and her sharp tongue that would slam hecklers, policemen and latecomers to the vigil with equal ferocity. In many ways, Hagar became the symbol of the vigil for us, and although disagreements with her would crop up for many of us, she always had our unflinching respect.' (Svirsky 1996: Ch.2)

6   A kibbutz is a collective community, founded on socialist and Zionist thought, and traditionally based on agriculture. Contemporary kibbutzim house not only farming but other economic activity including light industry and high technology enterprises. There are currently 200-300, mainly secular, kibbutzim accounting for 40 per cent of the country's agricultural output and 9 per cent of its industrial output. Moshavim are similarly cooperative settlements based on

community labour. (Wikipedia 'Kibbutz' and 'Moshav' accessed 6 June 2021)

7   This account of the Megiddo action, continued in the following paragraph, is from informal correspondence from Lily Traubmann and Yehudit Zeidenberg to Cynthia Cockburn.

8   Italian Women in Black say that a couple of days after this event, Marisa Manno, a member of Donne in Nero from Napoli, lost an eye due to being hit by broken glass while standing near a window in her hotel, near Damascus Gate.

9   Safran was sharply critical of Israeli WiB for what she called its 'erasure of lesbian existence'. WIB, she felt, did not use their potential 'to remain on the explosive side of society.' (Safran 2005:200)

10   Svirsky, Gila (1996) Standing for Peace: A History of Women in Black in Israel, online account at <http://www.gilasvirsky.com/wib_book. html> (accessed 14.6.2021)

11   An informative film Naila and the Uprising can be accessed online at <https://www.justvision.org/nailaandtheuprising/> (accessed 17 June 2021)

12   Lily Traubman and Yehudit Zeidenberg in informal correspondence with Cynthia Cockburn in early 2019.

13   The Aachen Peace Prize is funded by over 300 individuals and 50 religious, political, trade union and social groups to honour people who have made peace through a commitment to justice, non-violence, and civil courage. The prize-giving ceremony takes place every year on the 1st of September, the day on which German trade unions celebrate Anti-War Day. The name of the prize-winner is made known on the 8th of May, the Liberation from Fascism in Germany Day. <https://www.justvision.org/nailaandtheuprising/> (accessed 17 June 2021)

CHAPTER 2

STEPPING OUT:
WOMEN IN BLACK TRAVELS TO
THE USA, ITALY AND YUGOSLAVIA

In a matter of months:
to the United States of America

Women in Black as an idea and a practice travelled from Israel across the Atlantic to the USA with surprising speed. Jewish women peace activists in the USA were alert to developments in Israel Palestine and, like their counterparts, had been spurred into greater action by the outbreak of the *intifada*. In mid-1988, around six months after the Jerusalem women enacted their very first Women in Black vigil, the US women were replicating their action in weekly vigils in many towns and cities.

The Jewish population of the USA is believed currently to number around five and a half million, of whom at least half are thought to be non-observant. There exist numerous Jewish organisations including, in many towns and cities, Jewish Federations represented in a National Council. There is an overarching body called the Conference of Presidents of Major American Jewish Organisations (the 'Presidents' Conference' for short). The leadership of these structures, and of the four major denominations of synagogue (Reform, Conservative, Reconstructionist and Modern Orthodox) constitute what is sometimes termed 'the Jewish establishment'. In this establishment, as in the Jewish public at large, there has been a great deal of hotly debated difference of opinion concerning Israel, its government's policies and the Occupation of Palestine (Cantor 1990).

The earliest US Jewish women's on-street vigil was by a lesbian group in Minneapolis, calling themselves the Hannah Arendt Lesbian Peace Patrol. Their first gathering in February 1988, was just one month after the first WiB vigil in Jerusalem. Sharon Jaffe, one of this group, wrote: 'We wanted to see what would happen if we began to meet as Jewish lesbians' (Jaffe 1990:59). The same women participated in an organisation called the Minnesota Women's Alliance to End the Occupation, which was composed of Jewish, Palestinian and other US women, and together they went on to hold a weekly vigil during the summer of 1988 in solidarity with the WiB vigils in Israel, which were at that time spreading from Jerusalem to Haifa, Tel Aviv and elsewhere. Sharon Jaffe described their experience this way:

> Standing vigil is both scary and empowering. Scary because we are outside, subject to misogynist and homophobic angry men … The stress is counterbalanced by the empowerment of breaking silence and the growing support of women in Minneapolis and St Paul, women in Israel, women in Palestine, women around the United States. The vigils are both empowering and effective because women of varying class backgrounds, Jewish identities and sexualities, listen, consider, and begin to slowly, slowly and courageously open their hearts. (Jaffe 1990:60)

The creation of the Jewish Women's Committee to End the Occupation

A couple of months after the first Minnesota vigil, news of developments in Israel was brought to the USA by Lil Moed, a lesbian Jewish peace activist who shared her time between Israel and the USA. After talking with Lil, three US Jewish women — Clare Kinberg, Irena Klepfisz and Grace Paley —

decided to support the Israeli vigils. They called themselves the Jewish Women's Committee to End the Occupation of the West Bank and Gaza (JWCEO) and were based in New York. Irena and her colleagues stress that JWCEO was not, of itself, Women in Black. But its founding document stated that it had come into being 'in solidarity with Women in Black and other Israeli and Palestinian women's groups working for peace'. Like those groups, they aimed 'to end the Occupation', and for that purpose to 'support negotiations between the Israeli Government and the PLO toward the establishment of a Palestinian State alongside Israel' (Coordinating Committee of the JWCEO 1990:6).

JWCEO vigils, though they adopted the WiB 'look', differed in some ways from those in Jerusalem. Instead of choosing to gather at major traffic intersections, the women mounted their vigils in Jewish neighbourhoods, near synagogues and Jewish organisations, because their main aim, in those early days, was to urge their leaders to foster discussion on the Israeli crisis, and to attract more Jews, and particularly Jewish women, into activism around the issue. In New York, for instance, their vigil started outside the office of the Presidents' Conference at 515 Park Avenue. After a few moves, they eventually settled on a site in front of Zabars, a famous Jewish grocery in Upper West Side in Manhattan, a neighbourhood with many Jewish residents.

The JWCEO also began to hold regular meetings and to publish a bulletin — the *Jewish Women's Peace Bulletin*. Irena Klepfisz wrote that the bulletin:

> was not intended to create a national organization but rather to help women network and identify groups and activists across the country. We just asked who wanted to be listed and how they could be contacted. And we reported on activities. Many groups called themselves Women in Black. A few (not many) took [the name] JWCEO. Others just made up their own names ... We in New York specifically did not want to use Women in Black because we wanted to be visible as Jews.[1]

Irena went on to explain that their vigils were deliberately NOT silent. Rather, they actively encouraged dialogue and speech, even on the vigils, because they saw themselves as working 'against silence in American Jewish communities'. In their second year of activity, 1989, JWCEO organised some significant events. In January, they brought two activists to the USA from Israel: Mariam Mar'i, an Israeli Palestinian, and Edna Zarelski, an Israeli Jew. They organised a speaking tour of ten cities, during which Mariam and Edna shared the platform and spoke in dialogue about their relationship with women of the Palestinian communities in the Occupied Territories. A couple of months later, in March 1989, JWCEO participated in planning a conference in New York. Organised by mainstream rather than women's organisations, it was called 'Road to Peace' and was possibly the first event in the USA co-sponsored by an Israeli Jewish organisation (a magazine called *New Outlook*) and a Jerusalem-based Palestinian paper (*Al Fajr*). The media coverage was greater than anyone could have imagined, and the event seems to have appealed to the public to an astonishing degree: the list of those waiting for available tickets ran to 6,000. Women, however, were poorly represented in the conference, despite the best efforts of the JWCEO activists (Cohen 1990:66).

Later in that same year, on 2 October 1989, New York's JWCEO launched an action they called 'Days of Awe'. Groups in many locations in the USA and Canada participated. It involved vigils followed by speeches and performances about the condition of Palestinians in the Occupied Territories. They told of the hundreds of deaths during the *intifada* to date (including the deaths of 67 women), the many wounded, and the tens of thousands of arrests and imprisonments. They described the cruel conditions of 'administrative detention' in which some 1,900 Palestinians were then being held. And they reported on the aid — food, medicines, blood donations — that Israeli Jews and Palestinians in the peace movement were furnishing to the Palestinian communities with whom they were maintaining contact in the Occupied Territories (Nevel

1990). A further important contribution by the JWCEO was publishing a booklet entitled *Jewish Women's Call for Peace: A Handbook for Jewish Women on the Israeli/Palestinian Conflict*. Its editors were Rita Falbel, Irena Klepfisz and Donna Nevel — and this section references the many individually-authored articles it contains (Falbel 1990). 'JWCEO's primary function nationally was to help people network and find each other in different places and cities,' Irena wrote. 'It was all very grass roots.' The idea was to encourage Jewish women to form clearly identifiable groups to make American Jewish dissent visible to the US government, to the American Jewish community and back in Israel. As vigils went on to flower across the USA some called themselves JWCEO, some called themselves Women in Black, and others Jewish Women's Call for Peace.

In May 1991 Sherry Gorelick was sponsored by the JWCEO group in New York to attend the Women's Geneva Conference for Israeli-Palestinian Peace, in the Palais des Nations, Geneva. She reported back in *Bridges* journal, noting that this was the first meeting following the Gulf War in which women from Israel, from Palestine (four women attended from the Occupied Territories), and from thirteen other countries had come together. The conference was not exactly feminist, she wrote, but was definitely 'of women'. Its final document was a strong call for international intervention — they supplied a long list of needed actions — to assist Palestinians on the road to justice and statehood (Gorelick 1991:120-3).

The response the Women in Black and JWCEO vigils received from Jews they encountered in and around the Jewish centres where they held their vigils was expressive of the fierce differences of political opinion noted above. Rita Falbel wrote, 'Sometimes people talk to us. Some shout and argue, some call us names. Others take heart from our presence, and a few join in. We're not a large group, but that doesn't matter. It feels right to be out there' (Falbel 1990:13). Clare Kinberg wrote of an occasion when they were attacked by Jewish Defense League Kahanists,[2] 'young guys in their 20s or 30s, fanatically raving about the Torah and Jewish rights ... screaming "You are not Jewish, you defile the Jewish people"' (Kinberg 1990:21). Irena Klepfisz wrote, 'Over and again, we were told that the vigil was not only disloyal but a form of collaboration with contemporary and historical Nazis' (Klepfisz 1990:39). Outside Zabars grocery, they heard hecklers call 'Too bad you didn't die in the gas chambers!' A major dilemma for Women in Black activists as the practice of vigils spread in the USA was that any criticism of the state of Israel risked being deemed 'antisemitic', and the critic a 'self-hating Jew'. Irena Klepfisz wrote, 'When anti-Semites use the analogy [of the Holocaust] their intent is to negate German or world guilt. But when concerned, passionate Jews use the analogy, they are also trying to express their outrage over Israeli action and to shake other Jews out of their apathy over the fate of the Palestinians' (ibid:40). Women in Black activists had to be careful to do 'both/and': to highlight the historic persecution of Jews as well as contemporary Jewish oppression of Palestinians. Thus, San Francisco Women in Black advertised themselves in the following even-handed terms:

> We are Jewish and Palestinian women. We are concerned Americans. We stand in solidarity with Jewish and Palestinian women in Israel and elsewhere working for peace in the Middle East. We stand in protest against the continuing violence of the Israeli occupation of the Palestinian people. We stand in affirmation of the right of both peoples to self-determination, a secure existence and peace. We stand in mourning: for those who have died, for the human rights that have been violated, for the moral values that have been lost. (Falbel 1990:63)

A Women in Black group in Knoxville, Tennessee, has organised regular vigils since 2002 calling for an end to the Israeli state's occupation of Palestine and its other injustices toward the Palestinian people. These vigils continue to this day, and they write of themselves:

Our vigil was modelled on the vigils of Women in Black of Jerusalem. We are focused solely on Palestinian rights, ending the Occupation, and peace with justice between Israel and Palestine. In response to continued Palestinian resistance to Occupation, in late March 2002, Israel launched yet another military operation. In response to this escalation of violence, we Knoxville area women issued a call to stand in silent vigil on Tuesday, April 8, 2002, joining Israeli Women in Black who had by then been calling for an end to the Israeli Occupation of the West Bank for fourteen years, no less. The first vigil was held in front of the federal building in downtown Knoxville, the same spot where weekly vigils have subsequently been held now for nineteen years. The initial call for a vigil was issued by Palestinian women, both Christian and Muslim, and several other women involved in the Local Alliance for Mideast Peace. Several Jewish women responded immediately and joined the first vigil. Ours became a weekly vigil and the sequence has continued uninterrupted since that Tuesday in April 2002. Lasting 45 minutes, the vigil is held at noon each Tuesday, in front of the Duncan Federal Building, corner of Locust and Cumberland streets, downtown Knoxville. Someone is on the corner, no matter the holiday or the weather. Numbers have fluctuated, ranging from just a few people to over one hundred, depending on the situation or event (such as our annual anniversary observance).

Over the years we have engaged in a variety of outreach and education activities about the illegal occupation of Palestinian land by the Israeli government: speaking to church groups, offering public film showings followed by discussion, hosting potluck meals, etc. We have sponsored or co-sponsored speaking engagements by Palestinian and Israeli peace activists, including at least one refusenik, representatives from Tent of Nations,[3] and Palestinian Christian clergy. We have written letters to Congressional representatives; we update our placards and signs depending on the current issue. We in Knoxville are a classic Women in Black group in appearance and conduct. We wear black, and we hold signs that let passers-by know why we are standing. During the early years, the vigils were silent — but as years passed, this practice faded away. Now the last fifteen minutes of the vigil are silent — or at least that is the intent! We do not engage with people who take issue with what we are doing or what we stand for. Occasionally we talk with passers-by who want more information or who seem to be genuine in their interest. One person hands out map cards or other information (such as a flyer on the Boycott Divestment and Sanctions campaign). These days responses are almost all positive. In the early years, we had a lot of negative comments, or comments that were pro-Zionist (from evangelical Christians). People have also been curious. At one point, maybe five or six years in, the bus drivers' union invited us to speak at a monthly meeting, so they would know who we are and why we were a continued presence, so they could answer questions from their passengers.

Our current direction is to make our support of the pro-Palestinian Boycott Divestment and Sanctions campaign more visible. We also strengthened our capacity to bear witness to the truth of the Occupation and the status of Palestinian citizens of Israel by helping to send one of our vigillers to Bethlehem in July 2019 to attend BADIL Resource Center's nine-day Course in International Mobilization for the Inalienable Rights of Palestinian People. We feel that sustaining a strong array of WiB demonstrations in the USA may be considered particularly important because, after all, we are protesting in and against the country that commits the most money and engages in the most propaganda and false reporting in support of Israeli injustice to the Palestinian people.[4]

As Women in Black vigils like the one in Knoxville spread to more and more locations in the USA, other women were being inspired to vigil against violence, militarism and war in countries other than Israel Palestine. The Gulf War in 1990-91 prompted many to go out on the streets protesting against US involvement. Two characteristic, and characteristically different, Women in Black vigils were held in New York (Cockburn 2007). One was the Union Square vigil on a Thursday. Most of the women were Jewish women and their message focused exclusively on Israel Palestine. In 2004 this group had two distinct lives. It had begun in 1988 soon after WiB in Israel started and, as there, vigils ceased with the outbreak of the Gulf War. But it had revived with the onset of the second Palestinian *intifada* in 2000, and by 2004 the vigil was flourishing, with around thirty women regularly attending. It was markedly non-silent. 'We just can't keep quiet', they said. Besides, they explained, since they were not into holding meetings, their vigil hour had to enable some exchange of information. The focus of their banners in Union Square was clearly on ending the Occupation — 'Israeli and Palestinian women say the Occupation is killing us all', one of them read. The group gave out informative leaflets about the situation in the region. Lila Braine said, 'It's important for people to see us there and read our leaflets. It's additional information. It helps to counteract all the misinformation there is about. It's important to stand out there and say that not every Jew supports the Israeli government. It gives courage to other Jews' (Cockburn 2007:59).

By contrast, the second vigil in New York regularly gathered outside the Public Library in Manhattan on a Wednesday. This group made no reference to Israel or Palestine. It was one of the

WiB groups that had emerged and spread across the USA in the early 1990s in parallel with the specifically Israel-focused vigils, with themes ranging from campaigning against violence itself, including local incidents of racist violence or sexual violence against women, to any outbreak of aggression on the world stage. WiB vigils are currently (2022) held in the USA in: Alaska; California — in Berkeley, San Francisco, Bay Area, Mendocino, Santa Cruz, Nevada City, and Los Angeles; Baltimore; Colorado; Connecticut; Detroit; Indiana; Maine; Maryland; Michigan; Missouri; Montana; New Mexico — in Albuquerque and Santa Fe; New York; North Carolina; Oklahoma; Pennsylvania; Seattle; Knoxville, Tennessee and Washington DC.

However, let us go back to Israel and see how and why Italian women were drawn there, and subsequently adopted Women in Black for themselves.

Italian women take the path of solidarity

Contact between Israeli and Italian women peace activists went back to the late 1980s. At the start it involved women mainly from the Italian cities of Turin and Bologna, with some from Rome, Piacenza, Padova and elsewhere, travelling in the context of a project they called 'Visiting Difficult Places', *Visitare Luoghi Difficili (VLD).* By 'difficult places' they meant regions where people marked by significant 'difference', for instance of ethnicity, religion, culture or politics, were living together in a tense relationship. Lebanon was one such country the VLD group were drawn to study and visit. Israel was bound to be another. This network of Italian women was united by the desire to seek new peace policies for the Israeli-Palestinian conflict, a conflict they saw as the most difficult in recent history. What was unique about the VLD approach was that they had moved away from a static pacifist intent to an active relational one — a 'path of solidarity', as Elisabetta Donini explained it. 'We are convinced,' she wrote, 'that conflicts cannot be considered resolved when one side imposes itself on others, but when the diversity of stories, of cultures, experiences and projects can recognize each other, reciprocate, and live together' (VLD 1988:5).[5]

Inspired by a difficult partnership: Israeli Jews and Palestinians

An early Israeli contact for the Italian women was Michal Schwartz, an editor and journalist associated with the bilingual paper *Derech Hanitzotz/Tariq a Sharara* ('The Spark'), who visited Italy in mid-1987. She was a member of the Israeli Nitzotz organization, the strongly anti-Zionist group that campaigned for an end to the Occupation through the radical 'one-state' solution: turning Israel and the Occupied Territories into a single nation with equal citizenship of Jews and Palestinians. The Italian women of the VLD heard Michal speak about the Occupation, and the cooperation between Jewish feminist / peace activists and Palestinian women in the Territories. She became a point of reference for them, putting them in touch with women in Israel, who they subsequently visited. They were deeply impressed by the 'transversal' activism they found going on there — particularly in Jerusalem. They were sure that cooperating with these women over a longer period would help develop their own thinking not only about this conflict but also more generally about the means of working with and transcending 'difficult places/differences'.

The first major encounter between Italian feminists, Israeli Women in Black and Palestinian activists was a gathering in Jerusalem in the summer of 1988, organised by a partnership of three Italian organisations: the Women's House of Torino, the Women's Documentation Centre of Bologna, and women of a nationwide network named the Association for Peace. They called it the Peace Camp. Two preparatory visits took place.[6] It was decided that the Peace Camp would be held from 20-30 August 1988 in a hotel in East Jerusalem (that is to say, in the Palestinian, occupied, part of the city) and involve three or four days of seminars on health, schooling, jobs and conflict, followed by visits to Palestinian villages and refugee camps in the Occupied Territories. The Italian women hoped that it would be 'a precious opportunity for comparison between experiences of women who in the daily life of a divided country often intersect without communicating' (VLD 1988:15), and that it would develop into something more permanent and ongoing between Israelis and Palestinians, such as a Women's House in Jerusalem. When August came, a delegation of 68 Italian women travelled, each at her own expense, to the Peace Camp in Jerusalem, to meet Palestinian activists and Israeli Women in Black. There they learned (Elisabetta Donini later affirmed) that Palestinian activists were fighting a twofold struggle — for their rights as women, and for their survival and political expression as a nation. 'Gender is not "other" to, or separate from, social and military structures. Rather it is central to them. Thus "liberation" (as women) and "freedom" (as people) are intertwined' (VLD 1988:3).[7] WiB too expressed a double intention: wearing black meant mourning the suffering inflicted on the Palestinians and at the same time the loss of the values of the Jewish culture.

Back home from Jerusalem, the Italian women adopted the practice of vigils in WiB style. In September 1988 *Donne in Nero*, as it was called in Italian, gathered in front of the Altare Della Patria in the Piazza Venezia in Rome, a powerful symbol of nationalism and militarism. And in October of that year women from many different Italian towns came to Perugia-Assisi to march in a pacifist rally. In 1989 and early 1990, *Donne in Nero* vigils spread to many more Italian locations, focusing on the Israeli Occupation of the Palestinian territories, the Palestinian *intifada* and support for the 'transversal' political partnership being forged between peace-minded Jewish and Palestinian women.

When the Gulf War broke out in Autumn 1990 the Italian Peace Association protested against the involvement of Italy in the Western coalition and sought to mobilise opposition. This conflict caused *Donne in Nero* vigils to multiply further, especially in the centre and north of the country. In 1991 and 1992, there were groups in as many as eighty or ninety locations. In February 1991, 400 women identifying as *Donne in Nero* attended a national meeting in Rome. A month later the Italian movement — for such it now was — organised a well-attended, and widely reported, multi-city vigil for which it gained extensive publicity.

A questionnaire to portray Italian Women in Black

In 1992, a working group of women from the *Donne in Nero* group in Turin got together to think in some depth about Women in Black. They felt that, in line with the feminist aphorism 'the personal is political', 'each woman who stood in a vigil became an individual protagonist with her own body of a direct assumption of responsibility against violence, abuse, war'. The true meaning of the whole experience lay only in the 'emotions, reflections, the bodies, of the protagonists'. They decided to send a questionnaire to the largest possible number of *Donne in Nero* (DiN) groups to create from the responses something resembling 'a group portrait'. They circulated the questionnaire to all the Italian vigils they knew about at that time — more than eighty. The findings of this study were gathered in a paper (unpublished) entitled 'The Italian Case: An Open Experience' (*Casa delle Donne* Torino 1994).[8]

The survey report is interesting for having garnered a sense of the kind of phenomenon WiB was in Italy at that time. It was clear that women of DiN were varied and heterogeneous. They were feminists, political militants, pacifists — some were religious. What they had in common was the need to express themselves to their own and other governments as deeply opposed to policies of militarism and war. DiN groups, they discovered, did not only vigil. They also frequently met for discussions, and some produced written reflections, leaflets and posters. Some groups refused to pay taxes destined to fund the military and proposed a programme of diverting them to social causes instead. They concluded that WiB was 'a very meaningful phenomenon still subject to development' (*Casa delle Donne* Torino 1994).

The many WiB-style vigil groups in Italy did not deem themselves an organisation called *Donne in Nero*, they *did* DiN, they *enacted* it. WiB was a practice rather than an entity. For all that, the women adhered to each other through their individual sense of identity, the subjectivity they experienced and expressed in that practice. The more important elements of the practice were fourfold, the responses to the questionnaire revealed.

First, the choice of *a place to stand* was significant. To 'overtly show their disobedience' the women chose locations 'facing' (perhaps 'facing up to' would express this more precisely) political authority. So they chose Parliament Square in Rome, and in other towns the vigillers would often choose the seat of government at local level. Sometimes, to signal disrespect, they turned their backs to the building in question. For instance, they 'cold-shouldered' the Parliament building in January 1991 when the Members of Parliament voted in favour of participating in the Gulf War. In the latter, the Italian government were themselves a belligerent, so the women were obliged directly to oppose their own state.

The second element of DiN practice was *autonomy* — each vigil was an independent action, and within it, each woman was autonomous. Standing there, she simply *was*: 'I, a woman, against war'. In other words, each woman made a similar choice of action — but that action may have expressed different feelings for each of them.

The third element was the *silence* maintained by the vigils. The 'I' was simply the woman's body standing motionless and silent. Women in Pisa wrote that they found silence difficult to maintain, it was 'fatiguing'. Nonetheless they persisted. 'We chose silence', they wrote, 'to listen better, in order to be listened to better.'

Fourth, and finally, *the wearing of black* as expressive of mourning was important. Of course, women are often against their will confined to a space of tears and mourning. Some of the younger women did indeed express doubts about WiB's black symbolism for this reason. But in DiN practice, the 'black' was knowingly converted from something individual, private and imposed on women to something collective, public and chosen, in order to 'transmit a message of rebellion'. As Luisa Morgantini put it in an article in the newspaper *Il Manifesto* in February 1991, 'today the black colour we are wearing is really our own' (*Casa delle Donne* Torino 1994).

Discussing the findings of the survey amongst themselves, however, it became clear to the women of Italian WiB that the element in their practice that had enabled it to endure over several years without losing meaning was something much more difficult to define and explain than these four simple matters of place, autonomy, silence and blackness. It was the centrality in their practice of a challenging, and therefore productive, *contradiction*: they worked with and for women on both sides of a conflict. They could not and did not take sides. This was what WiB learned from the Italian women's earlier experience in the project of 'visiting difficult places'. They came to understand 'conflict' in a non-violent sense, seeing it not as the attempt to annihilate the 'other' but as a hard-work practice of relationship with that 'other'.

In 'visiting difficult places' such as Lebanon and Israel Palestine, they had learned a lot about handling contradictions. For example: in thinking about 'war' and 'peace' they had come to understand war as 'outrage and negation'. Yet, if they were honest, they had to look back and remember their old political allegiances with the fighters of wars of liberation, for instance in Vietnam in the 1960s and 1970s. What should they think of that now? Should they perhaps frame their current activism not as being 'against war' but as being 'for peace'? The problem persists, however, and it is not just semantic. 'Peace', as a concept, can seem 'too easy', denying 'difference', suggesting a 'false serenity'. So, using their VLD experience, the Italian women of *Donne in Nero* attempted to frame 'the idea of peace in dynamic perspective', 'not as tranquillity but the labour of acknowledging differences among ourselves and differences from others'. In that same spirit, WiB became a space in which to strive to rework one's own identity and subjectivity in negotiating between political differences.

As they completed their analysis of the survey of Italian Women in Black in 1994, the authors of the report felt bound to concede that 'we haven't stopped any wars'. The State of Israel and the Palestine Liberation Organisation were still at loggerheads. The Gulf War had run its course. On the other hand, they felt that vigils in WiB style had become established as 'the most intense way of expressing a rejection of violence', and around this practice they had succeeded in creating 'a thin but resilient network'.

WiB groups started up in other Italian cities later in the 1990s, including Naples:

> Our group of WiB has been together for a long time, having changed very little in its composition over the years. Our background is feminism, unions, and mixed pacifist groups against the war and against NATO. We started holding vigils as Women in Black in the 90s, against the Gulf wars and the wars in Yugoslavia, and we organised material support for the victims of the war. One of us was in Palestine during the demonstrations in 1988. Though we were in touch with Luisa Morgantini and WiB in other cities and participated in meetings and conferences, we only organised as a group in 1999. Since then, we have met regularly, holding vigils and organising political events and taking part in projects, sometimes in collaboration with other associations. We have been to Palestine many times and to Iraq, Lebanon, Kurdistan, Serbia, Mauritania, and Colombia. It was very relevant for us

to 'travel to difficult places' and establish relations with the women and the people there.

Naples WiB had interests in other issues, too, which we felt were linked to our philosophy toward a world where the conflicts could be dealt with and solved without violence, with no social and racial discrimination, where women had their place without being offended and persecuted. Therefore, we started a collaboration with other Italian women's groups or mixed groups in demanding 'public water', against private interests in the business of water distribution in Italy; we worked along with other groups in our region, Campania, for the defense of the earth against military and industrial soil contamination; we were in the movement for the protection of the environment against climate change; and took part in conventions and demonstrations for women's rights and against violence on women. (Renata La Rovere email to Sue Finch, November 2020)

The Italian women like to speak of a 'black thread' of 'symbolic contagion' that linked the early Israel-focused vigils with subsequent vigils opposing the Gulf War. The black thread ran onwards, for Italian WiB played a significant role on the wider stage, as we shall now see.

Disobedient Women: WiB comes to the Balkans

So, yes, it was Italian women who had become active as *Donne in Nero* who would now carry the idea and practice of Women in Black to the countries that were emerging from the disintegrating Socialist Federal Republic of Yugoslavia (SFRY). North-eastern Italy has a common border with Slovenia, one of the former republics of Yugoslavia, which on 25 June 1991 became the first to declare independence. Two months later, women of *Donne in Nero* in Venice and its neighbouring Mestre region made a cross-border move to contact Slovenian women and shared a vigil with them in the town of Capodistria (Koper). Soon afterwards the Venice-Mestre WiB travelled to meet women in Zagreb, Croatia, which had also declared independence in June 1991 after a year of conflict fuelled by Croatian nationalism and demands for autonomy by Serbs living in Croatia (Casa delle Donne 1993:9). A further impact was achieved by the transmission of the Woman in Black idea to a group of energetic women in Belgrade, Serbia. This link was effected first by Italian women of *Donne in Nero* from Turin, soon followed by women from Spain, where WiB had come into existence as *Mujeres de Negro*.

A little history may be useful here, although there is no account that will not be contested. The 'southern Slavs', for whom Yugoslavia is named, had populated the region since the sixth century CE, but over time had become differentiated by religion, with distinctive populations of Catholic and Orthodox Christians emerging in the Middle Ages, loyal respectively to Rome and Byzantium. A substantial Muslim population grew over 400 years of Ottoman rule from the late fourteenth century. National movements developed in the late nineteenth and early twentieth centuries, leading to the creation of a 'Kingdom of Slovenes, Serbs and Croatians', which, renamed 'Kingdom of Yugoslavia' in 1929, survived until the Second World War.

When, in 1941, the German forces and their allies invaded, they found ready support from the fascist Ustaše movement in Croatia. The principal resistance to the Nazi forces was that of partisans led by Josip Broz Tito. When the war ended in 1945, Tito emerged to take political control, creating a one-party Socialist Federal Republic of Yugoslavia. Tito's slogan of 'Brotherhood and Unity' aimed to do away with differences of religious identification and unify all Yugoslavs. In this way a strong socialist and secular Yugoslav identity developed among a post-war generation that viewed nationalism as the past. It was not to last, however. Tito died in 1980, leaving a power vacuum. The USA and other capitalist countries pressed neo-liberal economic reforms on Yugoslavia. The result was devastating unemployment, a deepening of class inequalities and growing social unrest. Political elites in several republics invoked nationalist feelings to boost their power, and in multiparty elections held in 1990, nationalist parties prevailed everywhere. Socialist Yugoslavia began to disintegrate.

The war in Bosnia-Herzegovina followed the declaration of independence by Bosnian Serbs and is estimated to have caused 100,000 deaths and displaced more than two million people from their homes. This conflict was the first in which mass rape of women by opposing military forces was acknowledged and widely reported as an act of war, and eventually led to the prosecution of rape as a war crime at the International Criminal Tribunal for the former Yugoslavia, and its recognition as torture and a crime against humanity. An estimated 20,000 women were raped as an act of war (Magas 1993, Woodward 1995 and Silber and Little 1995).

These tumultuous years of the early 1990s were the context in which Women in Black began in former Yugoslavia. There was already a women's movement there. Way back in the 1970s, feminist initiatives had started in the major cities — Belgrade, Zagreb and Ljubljana — and formed a strong backbone of links between women in different republics which continues to this day. In the 1980s the League of Communists had introduced formal sex-equality policies. Men continued to dominate the Party bureaucracy and public enterprises, but Yugoslav women grew accustomed in that decade to at least the expectation of access to most forms of employment (Morokvasić 1986). They were therefore profoundly disturbed by the reappearance of an openly misogynistic rule threatened by the emergent nationalist leaders who came to power in the elections of 1990. In those elections women were no longer protected by the 30 per cent quota of seats guaranteed previously, and their political representation collapsed drastically (Drakulić 1993). Pro-natalist policies introduced by the victorious demagogues were a sign of new times.

The task of the patriotic woman, they made clear, was no longer to build socialism by her labour power but to regenerate the nation through mothering its sons (Bracewell 1996). The wars which followed the break-up of Yugoslavia increased the already intense militarisation of the emergent states. Many men of military age fled rather than be conscripted to fight in wars they did not support, and some were imprisoned. Many more men went into hiding. Others who were already serving in the military deserted from their units. In Serbia, in just a few months between October 1991 and the spring of 1992, there were around fifty protests by military reservists with an estimated 55,000 participants (*ŽuC* 1994). Giving emotional, moral and political support to these men who refused to kill was one of the practical ways the newly forming groups of *Žene u Crnom* (Women in Black) found to act out their politics, in addition to their regular street vigils: *protiv Rata*, 'against war'. Some of the conscientious objectors hid from the authorities by living in the *ŽuC* office in Belgrade, and several of these men became valued associates of *ŽuC*. 'We have formed a male group supportive of the Women in Black which gathers antimilitarists, anti-patriarchalists, antisexists, and gay-pacifist activists,' *ŽuC* wrote in the 1994 issue of *Women for Peace*. That volume contained an anthology of materials concerning conscientious objection to military service. As Staša Zajović put it in her introduction, they wished to recognise the existence, and significance, of these 'Different Men', men 'who share our antisexism, antinationalism and antimilitarism' (*ŽuC* 1994:2).

State conscription of individuals into military service has until quite recently involved only male citizens — and in many countries, this is still the case. The military has been not only a national and nationalist institution but also a patriarchal one, a ranked hierarchy of males, fostering a concept of masculinity as essentially militarised, and citizenship as being for men only. One of the Belgrade conscientious objectors wrote 'A radical revision of the so-called "male" culture is a necessity.

The man must dare get out of his own skin, so to speak, and reject the authoritarian patriarchal patterns ... We must accept the feminists' offer of finding a new mode of organization and expression.' Men would be looking, he wrote, for 'a true partnership of freedom and mutual respect' with women activists (*ŽuC* 1994:134).

Likewise, supporting men in their refusal to serve in the state's military has been a particularly attractive, even necessary, form of antimilitarist activism for some feminist women because it so clearly challenges patriarchal gender relations, relations of difference and inequality, and potentially acts upon them in constructive ways. So, in the early 1990s, *Žene u Crnom* and the movement of conscientious objectors formed a partnership they termed the 'Conscientious Objection Network', that would continue throughout the years of fighting in Croatia and Bosnia-Herzegovina and beyond.

Out on the street as *Žene u Crnom*

In September 1991 a group of Italian women from *Donne in Nero* travelled to the region on an International Peace Caravan organised by Helsinki Citizens' Assembly. During a three-day stop in Belgrade, they met and exchanged ideas with some local women anti-war activists, including Lepa Mladjenović and Staša Zajović, and described their *Donna in Nero* (WiB) actions in Italy. Staša was already involved in the Centre for Anti-war Action, an organisation of both women and men. The encounter with the Italian visitors confirmed her growing conviction that a specifically women's anti-war activism was needed. Seeing these visitors 'do' Women in Black in a vigil in Sarajevo (27 September 1991) moved Staša, Lepa and their friends to adopt this form of action. Staša later wrote, 'For me, that was a very powerful feeling, in body and soul. When I returned to Belgrade, I went out day and night to persuade women. I believed that it [the Women in Black vigil action] was the best form.' They adopted not only the style but the name: Women in Black against War: *Žene u Crnom protiv Rata (ŽuC)*. Their first vigil under this name was held on 9 October 1991 outside the Student Cultural Centre, a site that had become familiar to feminists during the preceding decade as a progressive meeting place. The vigils continued weekly thereafter, and a few months later relocated in Republic Square.

The *ŽuC* vigils were every bit WiB in appearance and behaviour: women only, dressed in black, aspiring to be silent and still, with simple messages on banners and placards. Staša described *Žene u Crnom* as 'Always disloyal', and 'Always disobedient'. 'In theory and practice, with our minds and our words, we dismantle the patriarchal triad: sexism, nationalism and militarism,' *ŽuC* wrote of themselves,

We choose BLACK to refuse to serve as hostages of this regime that leads war; we refuse to be reduced to the social role of women as martyrs and victims … We choose SILENCE because we cannot find words to express the tragedy that war has brought or to express bitterness and repugnance against nationalist-militarist regimes, first of all, this one in Serbia … Our silence is visible … an invitation to women to reflect about themselves and about the women who have been raped, tortured and killed … who have disappeared, or whose loved ones have been killed and houses demolished. (*ŽuC* 1994:17)

The vigils were subjected to plentiful abuse from passers-by. As elsewhere, the taunts were often sexist: 'whores', 'bitches'. But they also often used presumed ethno-national identity as insult: 'you're not real Serbians'. Sometimes the hail of words turned into physical abuse, as when, on 29 October 1993, a Serbian paramilitary unit, the White Eagles, attacked the women. But the Belgrade vigillers kept it up. 'Don't speak for us — we'll speak for ourselves,' they were saying (*ŽuC* 1994:7).

Lepa Mladjenović recalls that the women on the vigils ranged in age between 18 and 75 years. Their backgrounds and lifestyles differed greatly. Some had been active feminists for a long time, while others were participating in feminist activism for the first time (*ŽuC* 1994:6). Lepa, for one, found vigils hard at first. Looking back, ten years later, she wrote,

> I was very embarrassed at that time to stand in the street. I felt strange ... There was actually no tradition here of women standing in the streets against some political act. I knew about the Israeli women, about the Italians, but it was quite different to know about them than to stand personally. After weeks and weeks of standing, this missing element was found ... we created our own tradition, sense and language. (*ŽuC* 2001:12)

Soon the women decided to open an office in Belgrade — then the capital of the Federal Republic of Yugoslavia — somewhere they could gather, discuss tactics, produce leaflets and plan their street actions. The group was hugely productive. In 2001, they reckoned that in that first decade of existence *Žene u Crnom* had handed out more than 50,000 leaflets about non-violence and resistance to war. They had organised more than eighty 'Women's Peace Travelling Workshops' in twelve towns in Serbia. They calculated that they had issued more than 100 public statements against the Serbian regime and its war policies. And they had published eleven annual volumes of their substantial series of books, *Women for Peace.* (*ŽuC* 1993, 1994, 1997, 1998, 1999, 2001, 2007 are drawn on in this account). A total of 35,000 copies of the books were produced in four languages: Serbo-Croat, English, Spanish and Italian (*ŽuC* 2001:346). *ŽuC* also established and maintained contact with women's organisations in the newly independent countries of Bosnia and Herzegovina, and Croatia. During the war, keeping connected was not easy. The postal service didn't function, and the phone lines were frequently inaccessible. However, in June 1992, German and Dutch peace activists set up *Zamir.net* (For Peace.net), an electronic communication network which worked on telephone lines and with simple computers but enabled peace groups across the region to communicate with each other.

In London some years later, Lepa Mladjenović recalled the pain of the wars and the new borders they created. Soon after fighting broke out in Croatia, she had gone to meet a train from Zagreb at the Belgrade rail station.

We heard that the train was strangely delayed. The report was first that it was an hour late, then several hours. Then two days. I still didn't understand then that there was a war going on. An important moment for me. Such a sad thing — the lost train. I didn't know, nobody could know, that that train would be five years late! In 1997, I went again to the railway station. The train was back! But now it was from the *international* ticket window I had to buy a ticket to Zagreb, not the local one. This time with a tear in my eye! (Cockburn 2007:84)

Fourteen years later, Lepa added, 'Women's solidarity saved my life'.[9] Establishing an office in Belgrade enabled fertile interaction between *Žene u Crnom* and other women's initiatives that started up in the capital. These included a Women's Studies Centre, offering courses and activities focused on women's issues and feminist theory; a small women's publishing house, *Feministićka 94*; and an Autonomous Women's Centre against Sexual Violence that supported, provided advocacy, and cared for women refugees from the wars in Bosnia and Herzegovina and in Croatia, including survivors of rape. Both *ŽuC* and the women's centre, alongside other women's groups, highlighted how rape was being used as a weapon of war. Together they advocated internationally for women's rights, including at the 1993 UN Conference on Women in Vienna — the first and most significant event where rape was specifically identified as a war crime. Many of the activists in these organisations were simultaneously *ŽuC* vigillers. Driving all of them was a determination to challenge patriarchal violence and a steadfast refusal of any differentiation of people on the basis of ethno-nationality.

A 'Network of Women's Solidarity against War': annual WiB conferences

Žene u Crnom also contributed significantly to the growth of Women in Black as an international movement when they established the practice of holding annual international conferences. The series was preceded by a conference in Venice in February 1992 organised by *Donne in Nero* and attended by around twenty women from former Yugoslavia, amongst others. Then in July that year the women of *ŽuC* Belgrade organised their own conference in Novi Sad (Northern Serbia), which drew around fifty women from the former Yugoslav region and fifty from Italy. It was from this moment that they began to use the concept of a 'Network of Women's Solidarity against War', the name in which the first eight international WiB conferences were mounted.

Whereas the only non-Yugoslav women to attend the conference in Novi Sad, in 1992, had been Italian women, the next conference, also in Novi Sad, from 3–8 August 1993, was more international. This time the Network of Women's Solidarity against War involved women from the USA, Austria, Germany, Belgium, Greece and the UK. It was attended by 108 women and drew feminist anti-war activists from the former Yugoslav entities of Bosnia and Herzegovina, Croatia, Macedonia and Slovenia. Many of the women who came were inspired by and took back the practice of WiB vigils and actions to their own countries.

One of the important themes discussed at the conference was the matter of acknowledging one's own ethno-cultural 'belonging'. Reluctant as a Serbian anti-war activist might be, due to a feeling of guilt, to 'name' herself as such in present circumstances, *ŽuC* felt 'that is a bad starting point ... It is arrogant to negate the thousand bonds which inspire us or oppress us. Our belonging to the female sex is not a sufficient definition of our identity, for that belonging does not unfold itself in a vacuum' (*ŽuC* 1994:114).

Laurence Hovde, a French Women in Black activist, wrote about the role of the international Women in Black conferences as catalysts:

Participating in Women in Black's International Meeting of Women's Solidarity Network Against War was my first time in the Federal Republic of Yugoslavia. It turned out to be a powerful catalyst in my personal/ political understanding of what sisterhood truly means.

I did the international coordination for the next two WiB conferences; working closely with Jadranka Miličević, a vibrant committed *Žene u Crnom*/Belgrade Women in Black activist who had left Sarajevo with her mother and two sons, while her husband and father stayed on. I have so many memories of this time: arriving at the meeting sites with Jadranka with no idea how we would be paying for everything, but the meeting was essential to networking across borders; we knew one small WiB group from Europe had some money for us, then another had too, then another; which is just one of the many ways women's solidarity made it possible to hold WiB meetings!

I lived for nearly a year in the *Žene u Crnom* flat; involved with their various activities on a 24/7 basis. The flat was on the upper floors of a residential building. And we were lucky because the neighbours at this time were for the most part tolerant of the constant flow of people coming in and out. The flat was an oasis for people needing a refuge from the expanding xenophobic hateful environment. It was a 'safe' place one could discuss openly, get what ŽuC called 'counter-information' about what was actually happening in the war zones. This information was distributed locally and internationally via fax, email and publications translated in three languages, and every week we organised the

Wednesday vigil and workshops that would follow. Someone would always make a big pot of food to be shared with whomever was there; could be international friends, and young men hiding from the forced military mobilisation. Around the table the discussion was so thick with cigarette smoke, and so often interrupted by some terrifying news from the war zones. (Personal communication to Cynthia Cockburn, 2019)

The third international meeting of the WiB Network was held in Jerusalem in December 1994, the fourth in Vojvodina in the summer of 1995, and the fifth in Novi Sad, from 1-4 August 1996. The participants from Bosnia and Herzegovina played an important role because the US-mediated Dayton Peace Agreement[10] had halted the Bosnian war just a few months earlier. Much of the discussion at the conference was an evaluation of that agreement. The cessation of hostilities had been hugely welcome. But the women deplored the way the US-led Dayton negotiators had carved Bosnia and Herzegovina into three ethnically distinct parts — Bosniak (Bosnian Muslim), Bosnian Serb and Bosnian Croat — causing further mass displacements. The key signatories to the agreement were, of course, the very same nationalist leaders who had brought about the wars. They were 'more like accomplices than enemies' (ŽuC 1997:31). Their agreement had simply embodied their nationalist motivations. The last of the series of annual international conferences organised by ŽuC was in August 2001, just a few months after Women in Black was awarded the Millennium Peace Prize by UNIFEM, which ŽuC Belgrade accepted on behalf of the WiB international network.

ŽuC have never stopped protesting against militarism and nationalism, and continue to be attacked for this, as they describe on their website and in leaflets:

On 9th October 1991, we began a public non-violent protest against the war; the Serbian regime's policy;

nationalism; militarism and all forms of hatred, discrimination and violence. Thus far, we have organized more than 500 protests, most of which took place in Belgrade streets and squares, but also in other cities of Serbia and Montenegro, throughout the former Yugoslavia, many cities of Europe, and around the world. Anti-militarism and non-violence are our spiritual orientation and our political choice. We reject military power and the production of arms for the killing of people, and for the domination of one sex, nation, or state over another. We speak out for recognition of difference, reciprocity, respect for nature, and for development in accordance with the needs of the civil population, and not the civil and military oligarchy and their national interests.[11]

We will never forget the Srebrenica genocide!

On 10 July 2021, on the 26th anniversary of the Srebrenica genocide, Women in Black held a protest with the slogan *"We will never forget the Srebrenica genocide"* in Republic Square, Belgrade. The Srebrenica genocide took place from 11 to 22 July 1995. 8,372 Bosniak men aged between 12 and 77 were killed in the genocide. Sites of mass executions: Jadar, Cerska, Tišća, Grbavci, Orahovac, Pilica, Branjevo. Over 20,000 members of Serb armed formations took part in the genocide. The remains of the killed were found in over 60 mass graves. (Women in Black Belgrade leaflet 15.7.2021)

The protest was attended by seventy activists from Belgrade, Novi Sad, Leskovac, Vlasotince, Kraljevo, Zrenjanin, Novi Pazar, Niš, and Pančevo, facing over seventy fascists shouting sexual insults and death threats.

Responding to war in Kosovo/a

To return to the summer of 1997, when the sixth international WiB conference was held — at that moment, another Yugoslav war was pending. In the south of Yugoslavia, adjacent to Albania, is a province that was home to a people of Albanian culture and language. Kosovo is its name in Serbian, Kosova in the Albanian language. From the late 1980s Serbia had increasingly repressed Albanian political and cultural institutions, revoking the province's autonomy in 1989, and declaring a state of emergency in 1990. Kosovo/a declared independence in 1991, embarking on a strategy of non-violent resistance. However, by 1996, this strategy was increasingly challenged by the Kosovan Liberation Army (KLA), funded by the Kosovar diaspora. At that sixth WiB conference, a message was read out to the assembled women from Nora Ahmetaj in Priština (Prishtinë), capital of Kosovo/a. She wrote, 'Serbs are my friends, they are the best to me in the world, but those here are monsters' (ŽuC 1997:123). One year later, in August 1998, by the time of the seventh conference, this time on Lake Palić, near Subotica, armed conflict between the KLA and Serbian police, military and paramilitary forces had been underway for six months. The conference issued an 'open letter' entitled 'We Refuse the War', demanding complete disarmament of all armed parties in Kosovo/a, the involvement of women in peace negotiations, and the trial of the leaders responsible for the conflict in the International Criminal Court (ŽuC 1999:120).

Now Žene u Crnom focused their weekly actions in Belgrade, issuing leaflets and public statements condemning the 'massive and brutal violations of individual and collective human rights of the citizens of Albanian nationality'. They called on Yugoslav soldiers and Serbian police to refuse service in Kosovo/a. They encouraged the nonviolent movement in Kosovo/a, and tried in every way possible to maintain connection with Kosovar Albanian women. But it was exceedingly difficult to reach them, beset as they were by Serbian police and the Yugoslav army. One Belgrade woman wrote at this time, 'My moral and emotional imperative (no matter how pathetic it sounds) is to spend hours and hours trying to get a phone line to Priština' (ŽuC 1999:183). The 1998 volume of Women for Peace is dominated by the Kosovo/a conflict, and carries several articles by Kosovar women, including Nora Ahmetaj and Nazlie Bala, the coordinator of ELENA, a women's human rights centre in Priština. It mentions visits made to Kosovo/a at this time, despite the violence, by some of the Belgrade WiB (*ŽuC* 1998). Addressing a conference in Struga, Macedonia, organised jointly by *Žene u Crnom* and a network of Kosovar women, Staša Zajović said, 'Once again, here before you, I repeat to the women with Albanian names, "Forgive us!" For the loss of your dearest, for endless humiliations, for indescribable pain and immeasurable suffering inflicted by the regime of the country we come from' (*ŽuC* 2007:5).

When the international offensive led by NATO forces began bombing Belgrade and other parts of the country, including Serbian targets in Kosovo, in March 1999, *ŽuC* joined forces with the Autonomous Women's Centre and turned their attention to setting up what they called a 'fear counselling team'. Using phone lines to maintain contact with women elsewhere, they helped each other overcome the panic caused by the bombardments. They later reported that in the first 25 days, five telephone counsellors had 378 phone sessions with women in 34 towns (*ŽuC* 1999:222).

Many Women in Black in western countries were appalled by the intervention of NATO forces and felt driven to demonstrate against their own militaries. *Žene u Crnom* and other women's organisations in Belgrade and the region were divided in their feelings and their responses in this new situation. On the one hand, they were appalled by the Serb forces' attack on the Kosovans. On the other, they were shaken by NATO aggression.[12] They felt caught, as they put it, between 'Milosević on the ground and NATO in the air'. After intensive discussion, *ŽuC* decided to refuse to condemn the NATO bombing, which had of course been condemned by their government. 'So long as we can't condemn our regime we won't condemn NATO. By all means do this for us!' (*ŽuC* 1999:27).[13]

ŽuC went on to inspire women in many other countries, including the UK — as we shall see in the next chapter.

NOTES

1   This paragraph, the preceding one and the two immediately following, draw on a personal e-mail between Irena Klepfisz and Cynthia Cockburn on 28 January 2019.

2   Followers of Rabbi Meir Kahane, an American-born Israeli, ordained Orthodox Rabbi, writer, and ultra-nationalist politician who started the Jewish Defense League in the US in 1968.

3   Tent of Nations is an educational and environmental farm near Bethlehem that has battled to protect their property from confiscation by the Israeli government for 25 years. They are a symbol of peace, farming their land and welcoming guests and volunteers of all nationalities and religions.

4   For more information about current WiB Knoxville events see https://www.facebook.com/WiBTennessee/Knoxville (accessed 17 June 2021)

5   The account that follows of Italian women's early contacts with Israeli and Palestinian women is drawn from an unpublished paper, obtained online, titled Visitare Luoghi Difficili 2, authored by the three participating groups: Casa delle Donne di Torino, Donne Dell'Associazione per la Pace and the Centro Delle Donne di Bologna. The short quotes are translations by Cynthia Cockburn. The page numbers cited relate to the Italian language pdf file. This paper is referred to as 'VLD 1988' here.

6   First, Caterina Ronco, Laura Scagliotti and Jolanda Bonino travelled to the region in the summer of 1987; while Caterina Ronco and Carla Ortona attended the second meeting in March 1988. They established multiple relations with both Jewish and Palestinian women, including Palestinian women from the Occupied Territories. This was the Italian women's earliest contact with Women in Black in Jerusalem.

7   Following the 1988 Jerusalem Peace Camp the Italian women went on to run a project of 'sponsorship' of Palestinian girls. They organized this in partnership with the several Palestinian women's committees associated with the Palestinian Union of Working Women's Committees (PUWWC). The project involved recruiting Italians, each willing to make a regular donation of money to a particular Palestinian family in support of an individual child. In addition to the monetary sponsorship, on three successive years from 1989 the project brought groups of the children, accompanied by Palestinian women leaders,

to visit holiday locations in Italy. They evaluated this activity in 1992 — though with some disappointment. They found it impossible to determine whether it had had a useful effect on the participants. And it left them with a certain sadness as they belatedly recognized that the initiative, largely developed as a charitable programme, was unsuitable for the feminist and political project they really aspired to be. However, among the results of the relationships established with Palestinian women and girls, it was relevant to have strengthened their status in the family and in society. According to the opinion of the Italian women who took care of the project, it was — at least in several cases — a small but important contribution to the empowerment process that was within their purposes.

8   The research was prompted by an invitation to the Italian women from Israeli Women in Black to contribute an article to a forthcoming book. The book project, however, did not materialise. Elisabetta Donini and Margherita Granero in an email to Cynthia Cockburn, 23 January 2019.

9   Lepa Mladjenović, in Feminist peace — opposing violence, militarism and war webinar 31.8.2021

10   The Dayton Peace Agreement was agreed 1 November 1995 at the Dayton airbase in Ohio, and formally signed in Paris on 14 December 1995.

11   \www.womeninblack.org/vigils/serbia (accessed 8.8.2021)

12   Women in Black Belgrade leaflet emailed to international WiB list, 15.7.2021

13   There was considerable tension in these years in and between feminist activist groups, some of a more nationalist and others of an anti-nationalist political orientation, over the issue of blame for the rape of women in the several Yugoslav conflicts. Some were inclined to pin blame on perpetrators of a particular ethnic group, while others took a more gender-based view, seeing rape not as predation determined by ethnic identity, but as a worldwide war of men against women. The various positionings and their implications are described in detail by Ana Miškovska Kajevska. (Miškovska 2017)

14   The international armed conflict ended in June 1999, with the withdrawal of the Serbian army from Kosovo/a, and the subsequent establishment of a temporary United Nations administration there. There has been no final resolution to the conflict, and while Kosovo formally remains part of Serbia under UN SC Resolution 1244/99, Kosovo declared unilateral independence in February 2008, and is currently recognised by 97 out of 193 United Nations member states https://worldpopulationreview.com/country-rankings/countries-that-recognize-kosovo (accessed 8.8.2021).

CHAPTER 3

WOMEN IN BLACK UK

When the war broke out in former Yugoslavia in 1991, I joined other Greenham women protesting, calling ourselves Women against War. This group evolved into Women in Black in solidarity with women protesting in Belgrade who had adopted the form of protest from Women in Black Israel/Palestine. (Liz Khan, London WiB)

Heartbreakingly, Cynthia did not live long enough to start on this chapter, so it was written by some WiB in the UK who were friends of Cynthia, including Liz Khan, Siân Jones, Rebecca Johnson, Sue Finch and many others; we invited WiB groups across the UK to contribute, and have quoted freely from their responses.

Cynthia wrote:

When you stand in silent vigil for an hour you have time to think. And one day in autumn of 1993 as I stood with other 'Women in Black' on the steps of St Martin's Church in central London in our weekly demonstration [...] I found myself thinking: we need to know more about *how peace is done*. I mean really *done*. Not how politicians posture, demand and concede. Not how people tolerate each other by muffling their disagreements and turning a blind eye to their injustices. But how some ordinary people arrange to fill the space between their national differences with words in place of bullets. What do they say to each other then?

We ourselves had had difficulty in agreeing the words we would display on our placards and banners ... although we all deplored aggression [...]. We had different points of political departure, some in the movement of principled pacifism, some in anti-racism or solidarity movements. We also came from different feminisms. (Cockburn 1998:1)

This chapter examines the different ways in which Women in Black (WiB) in the UK 'do peace'. It traces WiB UK's antecedents in feminist peace and anti-nuclear campaigns, and follows WiB from early beginnings in London, to the spread of vigils across the UK and current campaigns against militarism and violence against women. We look at how WiB moved from vigils to other forms of action against militarism, war, and the UK's nuclear weapons, adapting campaigns to meet evolving challenges. Women in Black stand for peace and for justice. But it is more complex than that. When she first imagined this book, Cynthia Cockburn asked 'How do we re-state and advance feminist understandings of gender in relation to violence and war, help eliminate violence against women and end militarism and war?' We examine that question from the standpoint of Women in Black in the UK.

Beginnings

In 1988, some of the women who later formed Women in Black stood in protest outside the London offices of the Israeli airline, El Al. They were standing in solidarity with Israeli and Palestinian women who had taken the name Women in Black in February 1988 to protest the 20-year occupation of Palestine.

Three years later in 1991 they came together with women from the Women's International League for Peace and Freedom, Greenham Women's Peace Camp and Act Together[1] to demonstrate against the first Gulf War on Iraq. They adopted the name Women in Black and campaigned against sanctions on Iraq.

WiB London also focussed on the wars tearing apart the then 'Federal Republic of Yugoslavia'. The group included Women's Aid to Former Yugoslavia, which had brought UK feminists into direct connection with WiB Belgrade; opponents of the occupation of Palestine, inspired by continuing WiB vigils in Jerusalem; and Women Against War Crimes, campaigning against sexual violence in war.

In 2001, as US and UK militarism escalated into wars on Afghanistan and Iraq after the '9/11' attacks, a network of Women in Black groups grew rapidly across the UK. By 2002, Women in Black UK's website listed regular vigils in the Bournemouth area, in Bradford, Brighton, Cambridge, Canterbury, Dundee, Edinburgh, Guilford, Hull, Lancaster, Leicester, London, Oxford, Manchester, Norfolk, Sheffield, Southampton and York.

While each group was autonomous, many joint actions took place. On International Women's Day, 8 March 2003, for example, just before the 20 March 2003 invasion of Iraq, Women in Black UK co-ordinated silent vigils at Aldermaston, in Birmingham, Bournemouth, Cambridge, London, Lyndhurst, Manchester, Newcastle, Nottingham, Weymouth and York in support of Iraqi women and against the continued sanctions on Iraq.

Antecedents and inspirations

Women in Black in the UK were initially inspired by Israeli and Palestinian women protesting against the occupation of Palestine, and by WiB Belgrade, as well as standing on the shoulders of a long history of women campaigning for peace and against nuclear weapons through the Women's International League for Peace and Freedom and the Greenham Common peace camp. Since then, WiB UK have drawn inspiration from and supported campaigns against war, and to end violence against women, welcome refugees and asylum seekers, oppose UK arms sales and support health and welfare spending, as well as the environmental movement to prevent climate catastrophe.

The Women's International League for Peace and Freedom (WILPF)

WILPF, founded in 1915, is one of the key antecedents for WiB in the UK, and shares the view that rape, forced prostitution, sexual trafficking and abuse of women and children increase during and after war (see Introduction). Cynthia Cockburn, one of London WiB founders, was an active member of WILPF, drafted their current manifesto, and took part in many WILPF actions. There is continuous collaboration in the UK between WILPF and WiB, supporting each other's activities:

> On WILPF's birthday, 28 April, we mounted a symbolic action outside the World Forum. Thousands of red plastic discs, symbolizing the world's $1776 billion global military expenditure, were piled in a heap. Women, with shovels and with their hands, scooped up the coins and transferred them to accounts of their choice — 'health', 'education' or 'human rights ... and put it to better use in health services, education, or human rights. (Cockburn 30.4.2015)

Greenham Common Women's Peace Camp

In 1980 the UK government agreed to base 96 ground-launched US missiles with nuclear warheads at Greenham Common in southern England. As preparations at the abandoned airfield went ahead, women in Wales prepared to oppose the deployment. On 27 August 1981, 36 Women for Life on Earth, along with a few men and children, began the 120 mile walk from Cardiff to Greenham. When they arrived on 5 September, some women chained themselves to the gates and fence, recalling tactics used by Suffragettes fighting for women's right to vote 70 years earlier; others set up a camp. While some of the marchers headed back to Wales, others stayed, determined not to leave without the public discussion they had called for; and the Greenham Common Women's Peace Camp began.

The Women's Peace Camp inspired a women's peace movement that was woven into the origins of Women in Black. Growing out of a tradition of British anti-nuclear protests and earlier pacifist movements, Greenham brought a feminist perspective to opposing nuclear weapons, and feminist resistance to the patriarchal attitudes and practices that dominated peace and political activities in the UK. It developed feminist empowerment, perspectives on nonviolence and opposition to nuclear weapons and war.

In early 1982, the camp decided that having started as a women's initiative they needed the few men to leave, so that they could move beyond male-dominated ways of thinking about peace. This decision was transformative. 'Men were asked to leave so that women were not in a supportive role but in the leading role, making decisions about the way forward. The actions at Greenham were often daring, and imaginative' (Liz Khan, London WiB).

Greenham Common Women's Peace Camp lasted nineteen years. The first camp at the main gate was joined by nine camps at other gates, each named after the colours of the rainbow, stretching around the nine-mile perimeter fence. Thousands of women lived at or visited the camp over the years, and the message that 'Greenham Women are Everywhere' enabled women from all over the UK, and many other countries, to join huge demonstrations at Greenham and take action locally. Liz Khan recalls:

> I was working as a childcare worker in a feminist children's centre when the call came out in December 1982 for women to embrace the USA military base at Greenham Common, that was preparing to host nuclear cruise missiles. A group of us from work joined the 30,000 women who protested that day. I then joined a local Greenham Common group that participated in actions both at Greenham Common and in my local vicinity, highlighting the evil of the weapons and

manoeuvres by the military both at Greenham Common and other military bases, including Faslane in Scotland. (Liz Khan in response to request for personal accounts from WiB in the UK).

The 'Embrace the base' demonstration in 1982 was widely reported on TV, radio and the front pages of many newspapers. The following day, over 6,000 women stayed to 'close the base' with mass blockades at seven gates.

Rebecca Johnson, a WiB who lived at Greenham from 1982 to 1987, adds:

> Whether in local groups or at camp, we set out not only to ban these weapons of mass annihilation, but to challenge patriarchal systems and attitudes at all levels, from the racism and colonialism at the core of today's wars, weapons and nuclear testing, to violence and abuse against women and girls. So many women came to Greenham with different experiences of sexual and patriarchal violence. Faced with violent policing and aggressive soldiers, passive resistance didn't work for us. To stop the nuclear deployments, we developed new forms of nonviolence, with empowering feminist-activist principles and practices to challenge and transform patriarchal violence. That's what Greenham meant — taking personal and political responsibility ourselves and changing how we live and what we do in the world. (Rebecca Johnson in response to request for personal accounts from WiB in the UK)

Women cut and pulled down miles of security fencing, entered the base, and occupied its sensitive military areas, including the nuclear silos and air traffic control tower. Convicted under the 600-year-old 'Breach of the Peace' legislation, or hastily enacted trespass laws, over 1,000 women were sent to Holloway and other prisons, proud to follow in the steps of the Suffragettes. After a 'Greenham Women Against

Cruise' court case in the US failed to prevent the arrival of cruise missiles in November 1983, the camp joined with local residents and anti-nuclear activists to form the 'Cruisewatch' network, which protested against and tracked every weapons convoy carrying missiles on public roads from Greenham to the deployment sites.

Within four years, the 1987 US-Soviet Intermediate-Range Nuclear Forces (INF) Treaty was signed.[2] By 1991, Cruise missiles had been removed from Greenham and destroyed. Greenham women and local residents ensured that Greenham was returned to common land for grazing animals and walkers to enjoy.

Like Liz and Rebecca, many Greenham Women became Women in Black. As Ann Jones of Portsmouth WiB explains: 'During the Greenham years I felt I belonged somewhere where I could do something about nuclear weapons [and] Cruisewatch was a practical role. I joined Women in Black to deepen my connections locally.'

Crossing borders: from Greenham to the Balkans

In 1992 a handful of Greenham women seeking to oppose the war in Yugoslavia contacted anti-nationalist women's organisations in Slovenia, Croatia and Serbia, with help from the National Peace Council, asking what they could do to support them. *Žene u Crnom (ŽuC*, Women in Black) in Belgrade replied with a request for humanitarian aid for women refugees, and so Women's Aid to Former Yugoslavia (WATFY) was established to collect and donate humanitarian aid and other support to displaced and refugee women on all sides of the conflicts, along with the activist networks supporting them.

In September 1992, after delivering aid in Ljubljana and Zagreb, nine women in three trucks arrived in Belgrade, met with *Žene u Crnom*, and joined their Women in Black vigil. Siân Jones, from Southampton, recalls: 'ŽuC's politics were a revelation: I'd never before so clearly understood the continuity of patriarchy, war, militarism and violence against women.'

Working with anti-nationalist women's organisations supporting displaced and refugee women, WATFY grew out of the Greenham network and several other women's organisations. Based mainly in Southampton and Bristol, they organised aid convoys until 1999, extending to Bosnia and Herzegovina and, later, Kosovo/a.[3] WATFY continued their close links with ŽuC and carried the idea of silent vigils and other black-clad protests against war back to their networks across the UK. They also brought new information about the use of rape as a weapon of war.

An umbrella campaign, Women against War Crimes, that included some WATFY women, along with a loose coalition drawn from a wide range of women's organisations, came together to call for war-time rape, already codified in international law as a war crime, to be prosecuted. The coalition activists lobbied, campaigned and with the participation of some women from the region held a massive demonstration in Trafalgar Square, London, on 7 March 1993. They joined the growing international coalition of women activists, organisations and lawyers who built global pressure for the prosecution of the act of individual and mass rape, sexual slavery and torture of both women and men committed by all parties in this and all other wars.

The first convictions for rape as a crime under international law took place at the International Criminal Tribunal for the former Yugoslavia, in 1997- 8. In a series of landmark cases, later Tribunals confirmed that rape was a form of torture; that rape and sexual assault may constitute acts of genocide; and that sexual violence, including enslavement or sexual slavery, could be prosecuted as a war crime, and as a crime against humanity.[4]

Women in Black across the UK continue to hold vigils opposing militarism and violence against women and take non-violent direct action for peace with justice. In 2022 Women in Black held vigils and took action in Borth and Aberystwyth, Bradford, Bristol, Cambridge, Glasgow, Edinburgh, Leeds,

Leicester, London, Oxford and Portsmouth, linked by email, Twitter, the WiB website, newsletters and a shared passion for peace with justice. They describe how WiB started in London and evolved across the UK as political situations changed below.

Women in Black: London

Liz Khan, London WIB, explains:

> The format used in the Women in Black vigils held in Israel and Belgrade was very similar to the protests we had as Women against War, e.g. placards and leaflets. Wearing black and holding silent vigils were something we easily took on. We felt that the silence was less threatening to the public and people were more easily able to engage with the one or two women who hand out leaflets and speak with the public.
>
> Initially, we were given permission to hold vigils on the steps of St Martin-in-the-Fields Church in Trafalgar Square. Then it was decided we should move to a secular space, the Edith Cavell statue, just a few metres away. This became the new home for Women in Black London, who felt that Edith Cavell's principles mirrored our own. The leaflets we give out provide information about the impact of patriarchy, war, weapons and violence on women.

Statue of Edith Cavell

When the First World War broke out, the Brussels clinic that Edith Cavell worked in became a Red Cross hospital nursing Belgians and occupying German forces. They also clandestinely nursed injured British soldiers, and connected them with Belgian activists, who helped more than 200 allied soldiers to escape before the network was discovered by the German authorities. Edith was arrested and executed by a firing squad at dawn on 15 October 1915. Her words are inscribed on her statue: 'Patriotism is not enough ... I must have no hatred or bitterness for anyone.'

London WiB vigils have been held every Wednesday at 6 p.m. since 2000 on the raised area around Edith Cavell's statue, which gives it visibility in the busy centre of London. The first vigil of every month is dedicated to supporting WiB Jerusalem's founding calls for building peace and justice by ending the Occupation of Palestine and working for an inclusive solution, upholding human rights and the security of women and children. As vigils are silent, women hold placards that always include *Women in Black against militarism and war*. The week's theme is also set out on placards and described in leaflets handed out by one or two women who stand apart from the vigil and engage with members of the public. Passers-by are asked to sign short letters, generally calling on the UK government to take action, which are collected in the WiB 'post box' and sent to the Prime Minister. Signatories often receive a reply, and many communicate this to WiB.

WiB London rotates vigils on themes of nuclear disarmament, resisting nationalism and war, preventing violence against women, opposing UK arms sales, divesting from militarism, and prioritising resources for peacebuilding, health and human security needs, including environmental sustainability.

Even before the attacks on the US on 11 September 2001 provided the impetus for the so-called 'War on Terror', the UK government was an eager US ally, with a 'Special Relationship' cemented in economic and foreign policy, joint military operations, NATO and shared nuclear technology. London WiB responded quickly to '9/11', joining a demonstration organised by anti-war groups calling for 'Justice not Vengeance' in Trafalgar Square. In the weeks immediately following 9/11, making links with other groups became particularly important for WiB London, who joined other women in a handful of women's organisations to co-ordinate an integrated approach to militarism, fundamentalisms and civil liberties, and forge long-standing links of mutual support. In September 2002, WiB London, along with Act Together, Southall Black Sisters, Women against Fundamentalisms, WILPF, and Women living Under Muslim Laws, organised a Women's Teach-In on Anti-Militarism, Fundamentalisms/Secularism, Civil Liberties and anti-terrorism legislation in Friends House in Euston Road, the central offices for Quakers in Britain.

In 2003, when yet another US-initiated and UK-supported war against Iraq threatened, many other women, like Maggie Luck, joined Women in Black:

> I hadn't lived in London very long and despite being a long-time member of the Campaign for Nuclear Disarmament (CND) had never actually been on a demo or taken any type of political action apart from being on the picket line at various places of work. Then I went on the big Iraq War demo in March 2003 with a friend of my then partner and a couple of children. What an eye opener that day was.
>
> After that I went on the second Iraq War march by myself and bumped into a woman I knew. I walked to the end of the demonstration with her and she asked me if I wanted to go to Edith Cavell's statue — wherever that was — with her, because WiB was standing ... So as I had nothing else to do I went (I would never have gone to a vigil by myself, way too shy — couldn't tell you how many times I'd driven past Greenham). I had heard of WIB, my partner had once shown me a photo of her on an action with them but that was all I knew about the group.
>
> I suppose the women vigilling on that Saturday were friendly, must have been, or I wouldn't have gone back! I particularly remember Liz Khan, Sue Finch and Jill Small. They were welcoming and I started to appear at vigils — which happily are silent. I find the whole

idea of standing in silent protest very powerful, I feel it is a great way to show strength of feeling — standing in solidarity.

Very soon after that I went with Liz and a couple of other women to leaflet an army barracks in London. Being part of WiB is a very important part of my life, I no longer live in London but if I ever happen to be there on a Wednesday I will make my way to Edith at 6 p.m.

As the frequency and intensity of protests against the impending Iraq War grew, Caroline from London WiB felt that there was no simple banner just asking for 'Peace' on the London marches. 'Peace had sort of got lost.' She used some money she had inherited from her mother — who had also been a peace activist — to take the lovely drawing that Picasso had given to the peace movement and have a quantity of simple banners made. The first major outing for the banners was on the Iraq anti-war march, when she and her family took many hundreds of the double-sided banners and gave them to demonstrators who would rather promote this simple message than any of the more negative ones.

Over time, WiB London has also produced T-shirts, bags, car and window stickers, flags, sashes, postcards, leaflets and information booklets as well as writing articles for *Open Democracy 50.50*, *Peace News* and other journals and newspapers.

Reflecting in 2021 on how the vigils have changed over the years, and the difficulties in attracting younger women to join WiB vigils, Liz Khan had this to say:

Our group is made up mostly of older women. We have made many attempts at recruiting more women over the years but have found that few women have stayed more than a few weeks. Our silence can appear unfriendly; our format can be restrictive and makes it difficult for new women to bring their enthusiasm and colour.

I feel that if we continue with the format the vigils will end when we all become either too old or too few to continue. I do not have an issue with this as I feel younger women have their own struggle and are doing protests in their own creative way.

A feminist analysis

Thinking about this chapter, Cynthia Cockburn considered how she could 'illustrate the wish we [Women in Black, London] had, and the difficulty we have had, in getting women and a women's perspective into all the various aspects of war and militarisation we protest'.

Some issues easily foreground women and invite a women's perspective. On International Women's Day, 8 March, every year, for example, London WiB invites other women's organisations to join a combined International Women's Day vigil, and also highlights women's work for peace around 24 May, International Women's Day for Peace and Disarmament. During refugee week in June, London WiB often join with activists from WILPF's Voices of African Women (VOAW) and with refugee support groups, addressing the rights and needs of women fleeing war and violence, or of refugee women detained for deportation in the UK. The International Day for the Elimination of Sexual Violence in Conflict (19 June) provides a similar opportunity.

Care is taken to ensure that women are not depicted only as victims of war or violence, but also as active agents in bringing about change in their own and others' lives. But how easy is it to incorporate explicitly feminist theory and politics into placards displayed and leaflets distributed to the passing public?

How do we convey the understanding of violence as a continuum — the violence that pervades the world — from domestic and interpersonal violence to violence within the community to state-sanctioned military violence?

London WiB always stand with placards which read Women in Black against violence; against militarism; against war. Our aims are clearly stated, but is the concept of militarism clearly understood? Similarly, is it possible to contextualise what Cynthia described as the triumvirate of patriarchy, militarism and war in a simple placard or leaflet? While WIB regularly support Reclaim the Night and Million Women Rise marches opposing violence against women, it has been difficult to conceptualise the continuum of violence between domestic violence and rape and the violence of war in a simple leaflet or banner.

So does WiB 'do peace' differently from mainstream peace and anti-war movements?

In trying to persuade the public that peace is 'more than a mere cessation of hostilities', we have reframed 'security', informed by definitions formulated by women and men in the global south. The military definition of security is replaced by a broader, humanitarian and feminist definition which conceives of security in terms of access to and enjoyment of basic human rights. WiB London try to present this alternative to military security, which focuses, for example, on the rights of access to food and water, to shelter, to education, to healthcare, to employment and the right to live without violence. This rethinking has informed the writing of leaflets in support of refugee, displaced and migrant women. Rather than present women as victims, texts foreground the agency of women and girls, for example in peace processes, working for the rights of survivors of conflict-related violence, or in opposition to the UK's arms sale to Saudi Arabia, by describing the impact of these weapons on women in Yemen, and initiatives taken by those women.

Feminist theory has informed our vigils calling for the scrapping of the UK's nuclear weapons system, and to use the billions saved 'for our real security needs, including health, education, poverty reduction [...], tackling climate change and environmental destruction' (WiB London leaflet, August 2019).

In vigils calling for peace with justice for the Palestinian people, WiB London rarely focussed on the gender dimensions of the Occupation at first. Did we fear undermining WiB's long-standing support for the rights of all Palestinians if we drew particular attention to Palestinian women's experience of domestic violence or legislation that limited the rights of unaccompanied women? Gradually WiB London have changed the narrative, looking for example at how the occupation has impacted women's health, or highlighting the struggle for justice by both Israeli and Palestinian women, from the testimonies of a female Israeli conscientious objector and a Palestinian farmer describing how Israeli settlers have tried to destroy her olive grove and thus her income.

Perhaps the most problematic vigils have been those addressing the 16 days of action between International Day for the Elimination of Violence Against Women (26 November) and Human Rights Day (10 December), focussing on the elimination of violence against women. London WiB has faced differences of opinion on how to address domestic or intimate partner violence, with no agreement as to how useful it is explicitly to call out 'male violence'. This difference is not about whether it is or is not male violence (it is), but whether the language pulls or pushes the audience. There is, however, general agreement with Cynthia that there is a continuum between violence against women in the home, and war violence:

> When we're looking for the links between war violence and violence against women in peace time, I think we need to look for causality, influence, flowing in both directions. Put briefly, violence in our everyday cultures, deeply gendered, predisposes societies to accept war as normal. And the violence of militarisation and war, profoundly gendered, spills back into everyday life and increases the quotient of violence in it. (Cockburn 25.11.2012)

Since then, the continuum of sexual violence against women has been highlighted by the #MeToo and Time's Up movements, vigils against the rape and murder of Sarah Everard by a serving police officer, and outrage at photos of murdered sisters Bibaa Henry and Nicole Smallman shared by police officers in the UK in 2021.

WiB extends across the UK

WiB in other parts of the UK have been even more direct about the continuum of violence: in March 2020, Borth and Aberystwyth WiB in Wales stood on a windswept seafront with a placard reading: 'Two women a week are killed by current or ex-partners in Wales and England'. Since then, there has been a significant rise in violence against women and rape during the lockdowns generated by the COVID pandemic. Less than 20 per cent of rapes are reported to the police in England and Wales. Only 1.6 per cent of the rapes that are reported result in someone being charged. Considerably fewer than one in every 100 reported rapes leads to any justice for its victim. At the same time, prosecutions and convictions for rape have fallen by 59 per cent and 47 per cent respectively since 2015/16.[5]

Women in Black across the UK, and across the world, campaign against the continuum of violence that stretches in both directions from rape and violence against individual women to rape and violence in war.

The sound of silence

Vigils are Women in Black's most consistent form of action across the UK. They serve many functions: some protest against violence against women; some seek to witness in silence; some to educate the public about an issue; some actively campaign for positive change, opposing UK military interventions or an end to arms sales, or calling out human rights violations or war crimes. Some commemorate or celebrate significant dates, like International Women's Day; other vigils encourage practical support, for example for refugee women or asylum seekers.

As the threat of war on Afghanistan grew in 2000-2001, so did opposition, with massive marches across the UK and around the world. Several more Women in Black vigils were started, including Cambridge Women in Black, established in 2002. Almost 20 years on, the Cambridge group continues to hold a silent vigil on the first Saturday of every month to protest against war, violence and the arms trade. They stand alongside those who are affected by war and displacement, those who are discriminated against, and oppressed, and those who grieve for the 'Disappeared'. Wearing black, to mourn all victims of war and terrorism, they are committed to a world free of violence, militarism and war.

In October 2001, women came together in Scotland to protest against the UK invasion of Afghanistan. By 2002, Women in Black Edinburgh (WIBE) had been formed and since 2003 have held silent vigils on Princes Street opposite the Balmoral Hotel from 1-2pm every Saturday. Other Women in Black groups have stood in Falkirk and Dundee. Women hold up banners saying: 'Women in Black Stand for Peace' and 'Women in Black say No to War'.

Here, in a 2020 leaflet, WiB Edinburgh describe the essence of their vigil:

'Peace is not the absence of conflict, but the presence of creative alternatives for responding to conflict.' [6]

While the women are impressive in their silence, one or two stand forward from the line open to conversation, even defence of WIBE's messages. We are subject to the full range of public responses, from approval and appreciation through to dismissal, lack of interest and disgust.

We stand vigil in solidarity and sisterhood — our ages span three, even four, generations — and each woman brings her own story. Women passing by are encouraged to join WiB even for as short a time as a few minutes before resuming their activities.

WiB vigils have spread around the world where women stand for alternatives to aggression and oppression, for peace and respect for human rights, and for women to be part of peace processes, wherever and whenever they take place. Women are powerful and if, like WiB Edinburgh, they are a threat to the status quo, these are values worth showing up for and standing up for over and over again — values of compassion, fairness and peace.

Since 2001, the UK has expanded its military activities in the Middle East and Africa in the name of democracy, freedom, and defence of its own citizens. WIB Edinburgh collect alternative news from sources outside mainstream media, and along with the visual impact of a line of women dressed in black in all weathers, a leaflet is offered to passers-by — informative, provocative, encouraging, and thoroughly researched …

We stand with all victims of conflict; We stand to bear silent witness against the futility of war and its destruction of human rights. (WIB Edinburgh leaflet 2020)

Other UK vigils focus more on Israel and Palestine, WiB's founding issue, as Carol from Oxford WiB wrote in response to a request for information about WiB UK:

The Network of Oxford Women (NOW) was established in 2002, and with the encouragement of one of our Jewish members, set up Oxford Women in Black (WiB). We mostly demonstrate in a central square and sometimes in our main shopping street, Cornmarket. It was originally once a month, usually on Saturday morning, more recently less frequently. At Christmas time we sing Alternative Carols relating to Israel's occupation of Palestinian land, the siege of Gaza and the arming of Israel by our government. Demonstrating as women feels very powerful. We encourage men to support us by giving out leaflets. We have links with WiB in Jerusalem and, through the charity Oxford Ramallah Friendship Association (ORFA), which builds grass-roots links between people in Oxford and Ramallah in Palestine, we have made contacts with women in refugee camps.

In other parts of the UK, WiB vigils focused on militarism. Portsmouth, for example, is a military city in the south of England, home to the UK's Royal Navy, with many residents dependent on the military economy. A vigil against war in Portsmouth is itself a visible challenge to militarism, and can attract both negative and positive reactions, as WiB Annette Rebentisch recalled in 2019:

> In the beginning we had a number of people reacting to us in a more negative way. There were also more people in cars waving, giving the thumbs up and saying they support us. The military police checked in a friendly, curious way, the local police, too, but much later and a bit less friendly. One day a woman asked us what we were doing. After we explained she said: 'I understand now, I have to see you as a whole, the posters, the clothes, you as a group of women. You are an icon'.

Annette continues:

> Sarah and I had attended the European Social Forum in London in 2004 and we decided to start something in Portsmouth in 2005. Sarah did the research and organising. She had heard about Women in Black and it seemed ideal for us. Its focus on women and on a peaceful, non-aggressive way to show what we believed in was what we had envisaged. Sarah arranged a meeting with two other interested women and in January 2005 we started our first vigil. I had always hated war — the Gulf War between Iran and Iraq that just went on and on because it was convenient, the Gulf War against Iraq after the Kuwait invasion, and now another Gulf

War. My third Gulf War, as if the world needed a Gulf War in each decade. The best way to show my anger was through silence. Since we started, the UK hasn't invaded another country. That's one good reason for not stopping. Another is that I meet once a month with like-minded women who are wonderful to listen to, who make me smile and laugh. One is a Quaker, one an artist and active in feminist circles, one supports the Socialist Workers Party and has been to Palestine.

We all have different ideas about peace and come from different angles. And that is fine. There isn't just one slogan and we don't have to agree on what we believe in. Which, to me, is what peace is.

Vigils in the Pandemic

In 2020-1, despite repeated lockdowns and successive prohibitions on gatherings during the COVID-19 pandemic, many Women in Black vigils continued, sometimes online and sometimes in the real world.

In London, WiB Pat Gaffney created a new social media template, which could be adapted each week to include an image and text for each virtual vigil. This was shared online, by email and on Twitter, and was used even when restrictions on protest were partially lifted, allowing only six socially distanced women to vigil. In July 2020, the virtual vigil highlighted the impact of Covid-19 on women in the UK where domestic violence doubled in the first 21 days of lock-down, and migrant women with no recourse to public funds were denied access to shelter and support.

In April 2020, seven Bradford WiB held a virtual vigil for Kashmiri women, posting an invitation on the group's Facebook page. Afterwards they met on Zoom: according to Joyce Robertshaw: 'We all agreed it wasn't the same as being with other women, but most of us had felt that just sitting quietly was helpful. Other women used the time to look up

information on the situation in Kashmir or listen to a programme about it'.

Edinburgh WiB held vigils from home for an hour on
Saturdays, putting a placard in their windows calling for an
end to armed conflict. One placard reads: 'Testing, not arming.
Ambulances, not tanks.'

In Portsmouth in April 2020, vigillers met on Zoom and
enjoyed being able to hear and see each other and felt linked
to the many women around the planet who are witnessing to
peace. Sarah Coote wrote: 'Some of us were at home struggling
with the novel technology and one was on a dodgy old phone
whilst doing a solo walking vigil in the usual place opposite
the Royal Navy base. The pictures of revolving trees and blue
skies were enjoyed by those indoors. It felt important to still be
a visible witness to peace in the face of the military.'

By 2022, most vigils were once more live.

Non-Violent Direct Action

We are not an organisation, but a means of mobilisation
and a formula for action (WIB London Information
pack, 2002)

While vigils have underpinned WiB UK protests against
militarism for over 30 years, WiB have also left their street-
side protests to take direct action against the occupation of
Palestine, war and militarism, including arms sales and nuclear
weapons. This has included action against UK military support
for NATO and US bombing campaigns.

In March 1999, Women in Black from Southampton, Bristol,
London and elsewhere demonstrated at USAF Fairford,[7] the
military airfield where US B52 and F1 bombers were preparing to take part in the NATO bombing of Serbia and targets
in Kosovo. After 24 March 1999, when internationally brokered peace talks between Serbian and Kosovo politicians at
Rambouillet failed, WiB protested at the front gates of the base.

In a powerful action, women read out transcripts of phone calls and emails from women in Belgrade in Serbia, from Croatia and Macedonia to their friends in Pristina in Kosovo, desperately looking for news, hoping that their friends and their families were safe, and searching for news about the impact of the bombing, trying to keep in touch across ethnic boundaries and national borders.

In 2001 five WiB from the UK joined the International Solidarity Movement to support Palestinian and Israeli women working for a peaceful resolution to the occupation. Some acted as human shields in Beit Jala, where 850 Palestinian homes had been shelled by Israeli forces that year, to protect Palestinian families from attack. They helped clear Israeli roadblocks, stood as human rights observers at Israeli checkpoints, and demonstrated in both Jerusalem and Bethlehem. As Liz Khan remembers:

> In 2001, I was part of a small group of women that visited Israel and Palestine. I participated in WiB vigils in Jerusalem and protested about the checkpoints that stop Palestinians travelling.
>
> I returned in 2002 with a WiB group and a film-maker, Donna Bailey, and a BBC Radio 5 team and participated in a film and radio programme about Women in Black. Once again, I participated in a number of protests including Human Shield,[8] staying in Palestinian families' homes that were being targeted by Israeli air attacks, removing roadblocks in towns and villages on the West Bank, protecting Palestinian olive harvest seasons from settlers and protesting about the building of the Separation Wall (separating Israel and Palestine) by the Israeli occupation forces.

In 2002, the International Women's Peace Service, founded by Angie Zelter, opened a house near Nablus in Palestine that was supported by some WiB:

On later visits I stayed at the Women's House based on the West Bank that had been set up to monitor human right violations. I joined checkpoints monitoring Israeli soldiers who were detaining Palestinians. Back in London our vigils continue to raise our concerns over the years at the continued blockade of Gaza, and the ever-expanding Israeli settlements in Palestinian territories. (Liz Khan, London WiB)

During the war on Iraq in 2003, WiB from Bristol, Birmingham, London and Southampton supported a peace camp at USAF Fairford and took action in and around the base from where US B52s, F1s and stealth bombers were now bombing Iraq. Protestors were stopped and searched under Anti-Terrorism laws.

WiB also joined blockades of the Joint Forces Headquarters in Northwood, London, a wartime command-and-control centre. On 6 April 2003, police 'kettled' protesters, preventing them from either blockading or leaving the demonstration. After several hours of negotiations had failed, four WiB deployed their bodies in protest. Taking off their clothes, they walked straight up to the police and soldiers present, asking for all to be let out as none posed a threat, just like those standing there naked. After a face-saving interval, several women, particularly older and disabled women, were let out.

After the Iraq war ended, WiB protested at an exhibition on Women and War at London's Imperial War Museum on a bitterly cold and windy weekend in November 2003, highlighting the museum's failure to include the history of women protesting and organising against war and militarism in the exhibition. Carrying WiB placards and banners, WiB formed a chain leading to the museum entrance, so that visitors had to walk past them. This prompted the museum's director to talk to the women and arrange a meeting. The Imperial War Museum now holds a Women in Black banner and T-shirt in their collection.

Sometimes I think of it like this: that patriarchy, nationalism and militarism are a kind of mutual admiration society ... and that ... pride in military service, the national honour and manliness are deep in 'modern' societies. It's there in the pro-war segment population in Britain today. (Cockburn blog, 2003)[9]

For some Women in Black, just opposing war is not enough. Militarism is the 'ism' that governments invest in during peacetime, which enables a country to prepare and be prepared for war and persuades a population to give their consent to war. However, militarism isn't a familiar concept in the UK, so Women in Black have adopted different strategies to show what militarism looks like, from working with the Campaign Against the Arms Trade and International Action Network on Small Arms — the global movement against gun violence; protesting against international militarised organisations like NATO; and highlighting how women and children are accidentally or deliberately killed by guns in their homes and communities.

Actions against the arms trade

Women in Black across the UK challenge militarism through opposition to the UK's arms sales, including protests at the government-sponsored Defence and Security Equipment International (DSEI) Arms Fair held every other year in London, since — bizarrely — 11 September 2001. The UK has been one of the world's most prolific arms manufacturers. In 2019, British manufacturers exported £11bn worth of arms to Saudi Arabia, the UK's biggest customer and one of the most repressive regimes in the world.

Since 2001, WiB have supported the Campaign against the Arms Trade (CAAT) against export of arms to Saudi Arabia. In 2019, the Supreme Court ordered the UK government not to grant any new licenses for arms sales to Saudi Arabia after CAAT revealed that UK-made warplanes, bombs and missiles were being used in the Saudi-led coalition's attacks on Yemen. The government had granted export licences for these arms without assessing their potential harm in violating the laws of wars, one of the conditions of their approval.

NATO

> What is our 'feminist case' against NATO? In many ways it's the same case we make against militarism and war in general. That's to say, we note the adverse ways they impact on women, and the damaging gender roles, active and passive, into which they draw both sexes. We point up the fact that gender relations, as we know and live them, are relations of power and inequality, founded in violence. They involve the social construction of masculinity as combative. Proper manhood requires a readiness to use force in defence of 'honour', while femininity is associated with passivity and victimhood. Women who want to escape the feminine stereotype have little choice but to imitate the masculine model. This dichotomous gender culture is one of the long-term, underlying, causes of war, because it predisposes our societies to see taking up arms as a normal and acceptable way of dealing with political conflicts. Consequently, feminist activists call for the transformation of gender relations as a necessary element of the movement to end war. (Cockburn September 2010)

Working with activists across Europe, WiB UK organises resistance to NATO:

> All of us are well-practised at campaigning for 'less military spending', 'No Trident', 'no to the arms trade' and 'troops out' of here and there. Now we are trying to frame our resistance to home-grown British militarism within a closer monitoring of trends in NATO and their implications for women's 'real security', rights and freedoms. (Cockburn 24/11/2010)[10]

The North Atlantic Treaty Organisation (NATO), a 30-state military coalition, originally comprised of the US and European states, had its origins in the Cold War, and a doctrine of nuclear sharing. WiB UK have often collaborated with Women against NATO,[11] who argue a feminist case for dismantling NATO, and against the militarisation of Europe. On 20 November 2010, WiB, WILPF, Aldermaston Women's Peace Camp (AWPC) and Trident Ploughshares women joined together to draw attention to the NATO Summit in Lisbon that weekend. Fourteen women, each wearing a light purple T-shirt, appeared on the streets of central London, standing in line, each T shirt bearing a letter (or none) to carefully spell out "SAY-NO-TO-NATO". Within three hours, more than a thousand people had taken a leaflet. 'What surprised us' wrote Cynthia Cockburn, 'was how many of them looked puzzled and asked, "What's NATO?"' Women supporting the action explained why 9,000 British soldiers were then fighting in Afghanistan as NATO troops; and how NATO's failure to implement UN Resolution 1325 included failing to stop the sexual abuse of women by 'peace-keepers' and failing to include women at peace talks. 'Women's voices aren't heard enough', commented Marie Claire Faray, a member of WILPF Voices of African Women, from the Democratic Republic of Congo, wearing a 'T': 'They ought to be part of the decision-making. They ought to set the agenda.'[12] The T-shirts (and some WiB) subsequently travelled to summits in the EU, returning to protest again at the 2014 NATO Summit in Cardiff, Wales, and the London Summit in 2019.

Since then, the Russian invasion of Ukraine in 2022 has led to a more nuanced view of NATO as uniting member states to support an independent country to resist attack, albeit through supplying weapons. However, it could be argued that one of the triggers of the invasion may have been Putin's fear that Ukraine would join NATO and become part of the continuing military build-up of NATO forces in Eastern Europe. Clearly nothing justifies the invasion that has cost thousands of lives and forced millions of women and children to become refugees, or Putin's threat to use nuclear weapons.

One of the many reasons why WiB in the UK has campaigned against NATO is that NATO also controls decisions related to use of the UK's nuclear weapons, so WiB London leaflets in March 2022 called for Russia, the USA, the UK, France and other nuclear-armed governments to join the UN Treaty on the Prohibition of Nuclear Weapons and eliminate their entire nuclear arsenals:

END WAR ON UKRAINE — IMMEDIATE CEASEFIRE — PREVENT NUCLEAR ATTACKS

Women in Black oppose militarism and war.

We recognise that many wars and violations of human rights and women's rights are taking place around the world, with and without the presence of nuclear weapons.

In the face of the Putin government's military invasion of Ukraine, Women in Black call for:

FIRST — WITH URGENT ACTION

→ an immediate ceasefire covering all armed personnel involved in this conflict

→ an end to the targeting of civilians, and use of illegal cruise missiles, cluster munitions, and all forms of explosive weaponry on cities and in populated areas

→ immediate negotiations to end the invasion and war

→ greater inclusion of skilled/experienced women and civil society peace-builders in this process

→ Putin (and his allies) and NATO governments to publicly pledge not to use nuclear weapons, under any circumstances

→ support, amplify and protect peace activists in Russia and Ukraine

→ the UK must welcome and support all refugees, from Ukraine and other armed conflicts in the world

FURTHER STEPS

→ laws on violence against women and children must be implemented, with more action to prevent and prosecute rape as a war crime

→ the connections between war, climate destruction and patriarchal violence need to be recognised

→ public campaigning to prevent future conflicts and end military-industrial profits, arms dealing, nuclear and fossil-fuel dependency

→ democratic engagement at all levels to limit the opportunities for militarists and nationalists to gain and abuse political power

→ Russia, the US, the UK, France and other nuclear-armed governments to join the UN Treaty on the Prohibition of Nuclear Weapons, and eliminate their entire nuclear arsenals.

→ the United Nations system and regional organisations need to be reformed and strengthened to work for the elimination of inhumane weapons, promote peace, human rights and justice, and adhere to international humanitarian laws

→ all of us need to work together for conflict resolution, war prevention, disarmament, the ending of occupations and colonialism, and the building of cooperative relations and real security.

Women in Black hold vigils every Wednesday between 6-7 pm at the Edith Cavell Statue, opposite the door of the National Portrait Gallery, St.Martin's Place, London, WC2. Our vigils are silent, women-only and if possible we wear black.

See our website at www.london.womeninblack.org
Contact us at: wibinfo@gn.apc.org
www.facebook.com/womeninblack.london
Twitter: @WIB_London

Creating Peace:
towards the abolition of nuclear weapons

As a Woman in Black, I have participated in protests at Faslane 365 where Women in Black started and ended a year of protest at the nuclear submarine base in 2006–7. I have participated in numerous actions at Aldermaston and Burghfield where nuclear missiles are developed and assembled. (Liz Khan, London WiB)

Nuclear weapons are perhaps the ultimate expression of militarised masculinity.[13] With roots in Greenham, most WiB actions have addressed nuclear disarmament, calling on successive UK governments to fulfil their existing nuclear disarmament obligations under the 1968 Non-Proliferation Treaty (NPT) and the 1996 Comprehensive Test Ban Treaty (CTBT). WiB calls for nuclear weapons to be abolished, for the UK to stop making them and for the use of nuclear weapons to be recognised as a crime against humanity and a war crime.

Over the years, WiB have joined with direct action groups like Trident Ploughshares in many nonviolent protests and actions at military-nuclear facilities, from Atomic Weapons Establishments at Aldermaston and Burghfield in Berkshire to Coulport navy depot, where the warheads made at Aldermaston and assembled at Burghfield are stored. Coulport, on Scotland's Loch Long, is just a short drive over the hills from the Gare Loch, site of the UK's nuclear submarine home port at Faslane, about 30 miles Northwest of Glasgow.

At least one of the four nuclear-armed Vanguard submarines based there is continuously on patrol at sea at any time. Current nuclear policies require that each submarine will carry up to eight US-made Trident missiles, each with a total of 40 warheads, most of which were designed to be eight times more powerful than the bomb that destroyed Hiroshima in 1945.

One WiB had a ringside view of UN and treaty developments: Rebecca Johnson was involved in developing strategy on the NPT and CTBT from 2000. From 2009, she was active in paving the way for the 2017 Treaty on the Prohibition of Nuclear Weapons (TPN). Rebecca recalls:

> I was sick of working so hard on the Non-Proliferation Treaty, and writing a report about Trident replacement, so I joined with Angie Zelter, and other peace activists from Trident Ploughshares and Nukewatch, to help inspire and coordinate a year of blockades at Faslane, 'Faslane 365', in 2006.

Women in Black and WILPF organised the first three blockade days, starting on 1st October. Over 100 women took part: WiB from the UK, and international WiB, including Rauda Morcos, a Palestinian peace activist from Jerusalem, and some from Leuven in Belgium. The first day was a reunion, sharing memories, food and songs, with workshops on the base, Scottish politics, racism and colonialism at the core of patriarchal militarism and nuclear weapons production, along with training in nonviolence and lock-on equipment, to pave the way for blockading to start. Helen John and I sat down to blockade, and got immediately arrested, taken to Clydebank police station and 'processed'. Over the day, 13 peace-women were arrested, each one greeted with shouts and songs. (Personal communication, 2021)

Later, on 15 February 2010, London WiB organised a women's blockade as part of a wider Trident Ploughshares action at Atomic Weapons Establishment (AWE) Aldermaston.[14] The blockade included activists from around Europe and Nobel Laureates Mairead Macguire (who founded Women for Peace in Northern Ireland) and Jody Williams. Banners called for: *Spend money on services not nuclear weapons*, and *No fists, no knives, no guns, no bombs — no to all violence*, identifying the continuum of violence, militarism and war. Several women locked on to blocks of concrete and successfully stopped traffic entering the Gate for several hours.

At the same time, WiB and Trident Ploughshares projected 'Stop Trident' and 'Trident is a War Crime' onto the Houses of Parliament and Ministry of Defence in London.

A few miles from Aldermaston at AWE Burghfield, WiB took part in blockades and actions as part of Action AWE in 2013, joined by international protesters from France, Belgium, Sweden, Spain, Japan and UK to close Burghfield for over a day. Liz Khan remembers: 'We slept in the Friends Meeting House in Reading and got to Burghfield and "locked-on" in freezing temperatures before dawn. There was singing, a band, dancing and theatre and a paper mâché nuclear missile that exploded with lots of confetti simulating radiation.'

On 9 August — Nagasaki Day — in 2014, WiB joined AWPC, ICAN, CND, Action AWE and other activists to connect the Aldermaston and Burghfield bomb factories with a seven-mile pink peace scarf to protest against renewing Trident, The *Wool against Weapons* peace scarf was made by sewing together thousands of wool rectangles knitted by women, men and children from all over the UK and other countries. The scarf reappeared at a 'Wrap up Trident' demonstration at the Houses of Parliament in 2015 and was then repurposed into blankets and donated to organisations supporting refugees and asylum seekers.

Not silent, but singing

Following a 24-hour blockade by WiB at AWE in June 2016, on 18 July 2016, WiB and the Raised Voices choir, including Cynthia and other London WiB, came together with singers from around the country for a 'Trident: A British War Crime' Oratorio in the central lobby of the House of Commons, composed by WiB Camilla Cantantata, and first sung in July 2004 by WiB and Trident Ploughshares singers at the Scottish High Court.

Banning nuclear weapons

Since 2017, WiB vigils in London and Edinburgh have called on the government to sign and ratify the UN Treaty Prohibiting Nuclear Weapons. In January 2017, the UN General Assembly (UNGA) convened multilateral negotiations on nuclear disarmament. These were boycotted by the UK, the eight other nuclear states and most NATO governments. Nonetheless, on 7 July 2017 the Treaty on the Prohibition of Nuclear Weapons (TPNW) was adopted by the UNGA by 122 votes to one against, with one abstention (Singapore). The Treaty opened for states to sign on 20 September 2017 and entered into force on 22 January 2021. It now frames WiB calls for UK nuclear disarmament. The purpose of the Treaty is to prevent nuclear weapons ever being used again. It prohibits all the practical activities that would enable both states and non-state actors to use nuclear weapons and requires states parties to facilitate the irreversible elimination of all nuclear arsenals. Article I brings into force clear prohibitions on the use, development, testing, production, deployment, stockpiling, acquisition and possession of nuclear weapons, as well as stationing and transferring nuclear weapons, thereby outlawing the nuclear sharing practised by NATO.

The Treaty is not just a symbolic ban. It requires the total elimination of nuclear weapons and provides two practical pathways for nuclear-armed states and nuclear alliances like NATO to comply and join. Both require states to eliminate nuclear weapons and programmes from their territories. The Treaty also places positive obligations and responsibilities on states, including environmental remediation and international cooperation and assistance, as well as to provide technical and financial help for victims and environments affected by the use or testing of nuclear weapons.

Indeed, as Rebecca Johnson describes [below], feminist analysis and activism underpins the language and intent of the 2021 Treaty on the Prohibition of Nuclear Weapons. The Treaty reflects its origins in feminist activism and analysis along with humanitarian perspectives and practice. It acknowledges the 'catastrophic consequences of nuclear weapons' and their 'grave implications for human survival, the environment, socio-economic development, the global economy, food security and the health of current and future generations', and importantly, their 'disproportionate impact on women and girls, including as a result of ionizing radiation'.

The Treaty recognises 'that the equal, full and effective participation of both women and men is an essential factor for the promotion and attainment of sustainable peace and security, and is committed to supporting and strengthening the effective participation of women in nuclear disarmament.'[15]

NOTES

1   A group composed of Iraqi and non-Iraqi women, many of whom were also WiB.

2   David Fairhall, Yossef Bodansky, 'Soviet Spetsnaz at Greenham', and 'Greenham Defenses Copied for Spetsnaz Training,' *Jane's Defence Weekly*, 25 January 1986, 83, 84. See also Duncan Campbell and Patrick Forbes, *Greenham Spies: More Bluster*, New Statesman 7 February 1986, http://www.duncancampbell.org/content/new-statesman-1986 (accessed 26.6.2021)

3   Other former Greenham women involved in the first WATFY convoy subsequently set up the Manchester-based 'Women's Aid for Peace'

4   Rape as form of torture; ICTY, Celebici, Mucic et al, 1998 https://ijrcenter.org/international-criminal-law/icty/case-summaries/mucic/ (accessed 25.11.21); Genocide: ICTR, Akayesu 1998 https://ijrcenter.org/international-criminal-law/ictr/case-summaries/akayesu/ (accessed 25.11.21); Sexual violence as a war crime, and as a crime against humanity including enslavement and/or sexual slavery, ICTY, 2000 https://www.icty.org/en/features/crimes-sexual-violence (accessed 25.11.21).

5   HM Government, *The end-to-end rape review report on findings and actions*, June 2021

6   Dorothy Thompson, American suffragist and journalist, *1893-1961*

7   The Royal Air Force base at Fairford was handed over to the US Air Force from October 1988, when a fleet of US B52 bombers arrived at the airfield as Serb police and military forces continued attacks on the Kosovo Albanian population, and the Kosovo Liberation Army fought back.

8   A group of Women in Black from the UK joined the International Solidarity Movement in Palestine to act as human shields in Beit Jala to protect Palestinian families from attack by Israeli jets and settlers. 850 Palestinian homes had been shelled by Israeli forces in that area that year. The women also demonstrated in Jerusalem and Bethlehem in the hope that the treatment of Palestinians would get international publicity (publicised by George Monbiot, *Hell's Grannies*, Guardian 14 August 2001)

9   Cynthia Cockburn, *Why (and which) feminist anti-militarism*, https://
     www.cynthiacockburn.org/Blogfemantimilitarism.pdf 2003
10   Cynthia Cockburn, 'N-A-T-O, What's that stand for?' https://www.
     opendemocracy.net/en/5050/n-t-o-whats-that-stand-for/ 24/11/2010
     (accessed 15.6.2021)
11   https://www.no-to-nato.org/women-against-nato/ (accessed 9.11.2021)
12   Marie Clare Faray, quoted in 'WOMEN SAY 'NO TO NATO'
     statement: November 20, 2010, http://www.wloe.org/London-20-Nov-
     2010.586.0.html (accessed 16.6.2021)
13   See, for example, Dr Helen Caldicott, *Missile Envy: The Arms Race and
     Nuclear War*, Bantam Doubleday Dell Publishing Group, 1986
14   For background to the blockade, see Cynthia Cockburn speech to War
     Resisters' International in 2010, https://wri-irg.org/en/story/2010/
     womens-resistance-aldermaston (accessed 14.6.2021)
15   Treaty on the Prohibition of Nuclear Weapons, Preambular paragraphs,
     https://undocs.org/A/CONF.229/2017/8 (accessed 15.6.2021)

Israeli and Palestinian WiB vigil at the international WiB conference, Jerusalem, 2005
© Lieve Snellings

London WiB International Women's Day vigil, 200
© Cynthia Cockburn

South African WiB at 'Break the Silence' demonstration, Cape Town, 2007
© Lieve Snellings

WiB Leuven at the Valencia WiB conference, 2007
© Morgan Stetler

South African WiB at the Valencia WiB conference, 2007
© Lieve Snellings

WiB vigil during Women's Court against dowry and related violence against women, Bangalore, 2009 © Lieve Snellings

Yvonne Deutsch and Nabila Espanioly, Israeli and Palestinian WiB, demonstrate in Leuven, Belgium, 2014 © Lieve Snellings

WiB Armenia, Yerevan, 2016
© Lieve Snellings

Poster from WiB conference in Colombia 2011 Photo
© Morgan Stetler

CHAPTER 4

GETTING CONNECTED:
FROM SPAIN TO LEUVEN

Connecting with Women in Black in former Yugoslavia inspired WiB UK and went on to inspire women in Spain and Belgium to start WiB groups, as well as a communication network that connects and spreads WiB ideas across the world. In the winter of 1992-3 a group of four *Movimiento de Objección de Conciencia* (Movement of Conscientious Objection)[1] men had travelled from Spain to the Yugoslav region to make contact with war resisters there. They were warmly received in Belgrade by the Conscientious Objection Network in which *Žene u Crnom* (Women in Black) were active. The latter greatly impressed them by their analysis and drive. The result of this contact was that in April 1993, Staša Zajović from *Žene u Crnom (ŽuC)* made a twenty-day speaking tour in Spain. As it happened, she is a fluent Spanish speaker, and this tour would be the first of several. Staša insisted that everywhere she went and spoke, she should be put in touch with women antimilitarist activists. As a result of her visit, many local women's groups, including those in Zaragoza, Palma de Majorca and Barcelona, subsequently took the name Women in Black — *Mujeres de Negro*. Soon afterwards, a number of Spanish women visited Yugoslavia to attend *ŽuC's* annual meeting, which was held in Novi Sad in August 1993. The group included women from Merida, Sevilla, Zaragoza, Bilbao and Barcelona. During the three days of meetings, a vigil was organised in the central square. One of the participants described it:

There were around 150 women from almost every part of the world. Italy, the Biscay region, France, Germany, Austria, USA, England, as well as from former Yugoslavia: Macedonia, Croatia, Bosnia, Montenegro, Slovenia. We formed a semicircle around the monument in the centre of the square and slowly unfolded our — mostly black — signs with white inscriptions in several languages ... We pause, take each other by the hand and form a circle which encompasses the entire square. Absolute silence ... All this elicits intensive emotions and leaves a strong impression, not so much on the audience — which is practically non-existent — as on us. (*ŽuC* 1994:87)

The Spanish group of *Mujeres de Negro* who attended this August conference in Novi Sad invited *ŽuC* women to come and meet with them three months later in the Spanish town of Merida. It was November 1993. Eight Yugoslav women travelled from an already ice-bound Belgrade to still sunny Merida for the meeting.[2] It was a very productive discussion, covered in several radio and TV shows. The Yugoslav women were touched by the warmth of the Spanish women's welcome. It was agreed that Spanish women would attend the forthcoming international meeting of Women in Black which *ŽuC* were offering to host in August the following year — 1994 — in Novi Sad. Staša wrote, 'I felt that our lives were intertwined, despite the different realities we live in' (*ŽuC* 1994:153).

ŽuC were already actively resisting compulsory military service and now connected with the *Movimiento de Objección de Conciencia* that was flourishing in Spain. In the amnesty that had followed the death of the dictator Francisco Franco in 1975, among the many individuals released from his prisons were 285 conscientious objectors (COs). The post-dictatorship Spanish Constitution of 1976 did not annul Franco's imposition of obligatory military service, but it added an important modification, introducing an option for refuseniks to undertake substitute social service. In 1977 organised resistance to military service had taken shape in the *Movimiento de Objección de*

Conciencia (MOC).[3] *MOC* from the start adopted the notion of 'total objection', by which they meant the refusal not only of military service but of substitute social service too — these full objectors were called *insumisos* (rebels). It was a popular option. By 1990 there were six times as many men in full *insumisión* as those undertaking substitute social service. As they came of age in the following years, many thousands of young Spanish men declared themselves COs. Not knowing how to deal with these numbers, the government devised yet another modification, by means of a provision that conscripts might delay their service. In choosing this 'deferred conscription' (*incorporación aplazada*) the individual would be put 'on hold' indefinitely. By the end of the 1990s this had become the norm rather than the exception. In 1997, four years before compulsory service in Spain was terminated altogether, the state received 130,000 applications for deferral of service (*MOC* 2002). When, in 2000, the Spanish state finally wearied of the struggle to corral men into the barracks and fully professionalised its armed forces, the unpopularity of the military was such that it had to make do with only 75 per cent of the personnel it needed (Zamarra 2009).

Although during the conscription years it was men who were forcibly enlisted, many women joined *MOC* because it was a movement not just against military service but against militarisation itself and the tangible effects it had on everyone's lives, including, in gender-specific ways, those of women. Not a few of these women felt a growing need to meet, talk and organise a dual militancy, to be active not only as 'people' in *MOC* but as *women* in *MOC*, women with a feminist agenda. *MOC*'s Ideological Declaration of 1979 recognised the issue of power and domination inherent in militarisation. The first paragraph of their second Declaration in 1986 included the following:

> *MOC* is committed to the struggle to overcome the present oppression exercised over women, empowering feminist work which develops in the organisation as

a rejuvenating and non-*machista* spirit in personal relations. Equally *MOC* is engaged in the critique and denunciation of the function of the army and militarism as transmitters and glorifiers of *machista* and patriarchal values. (*MOC* 2002: 305)

In this spirit, *MoC* soon decided that their name should be not 'Movement of Conscientious Objectors' (*objetores*, a male noun), but rather 'Movement of Conscientious Objection' (*objeción*). The war hero is, trans-historically, a key character in the patriarchal drama. An effort therefore had to be made in *MOC* to avoid reproducing the heroic male role in the person of the conscientious objector, the brave man willing to face imprisonment, engaging single-handedly with the judges, commanders and prison governors of the enemy state.[4]

Mujeres de Negro: WiB flowers in Spain

A fertile connection had been established between Yugoslav and Spanish women that would lead to women in many Spanish cities adopting the name and practice of *Mujeres de Negro* (Women in Black). One of the most active groups was in the southern city of Sevilla. During a research project in 2007, Cynthia Cockburn spent some time with them and met Mireya Forel. Mireya told her how, as a young woman, she had been a Marxist, active in the *Liga Comunista Revolucionaria* (LCR — Revolutionary Communist League) in Andalucia. But she had felt the need for an autonomous feminist space more and more strongly, something that was anathema to the communists. Mireya had therefore left the *Liga* in 1985 and some years later, during an anti-NATO campaign, got to know some of the *MOC* activists in Sevilla. Through them she came in contact with Yugoslav objectors and eventually met women from *Žene u Crnom*. As a result, Mireya and other *MOC* women in Sevilla set up a Women in Black group there. Although the antimilitarist motivation was strong among them, it was not merely a secession from *MOC*. Some 80 per cent of the Women in Black in Sevilla were young women from local progressive movements such as *ecologistas* (environmentalists), squatters and community groups.

The second woman Cynthia met in Sevilla was Sofía Herrera. Sofia told her how, in the 1990s, her son Javi had been a CO, and she had been active in his support group and in *MOC*. Sometimes when they were out on an antimilitarist demonstration, Javi would say to her, 'Why don't you go and walk with the *Mujeres de Negro*?' But at that time, she told me, these women had seemed a bit strange to her, with their black clothes and their banners. Then, one day in 1997, she met Mireya and with her encouragement hesitantly got involved with *Mujeres de Negro* (MdN), curious to learn more about its feminist and anti-militarist ideas. She told Cynthia,

> *Mujeres de Negro* in Sevilla was a small group, and still is. There were some young women, very vibrant. It was very different from other groups I'd known, the way they reflected on their actions, and on their interactions with the people in the street. It was a comfortable space where you could express yourself as a woman. In mixed groups, men have more space, more security, more power. In a woman-only group everything seemed easier. (Cockburn 2012:98)

Sofía told Cynthia how *MdN* in Sevilla had evolved certain working principles.[5] They decided on weekly meetings with occasional 'days of reflection' for deeper discussions. They also decided not to act alone, but to look outward for connections, for partners. It was in this spirit that *Mujeres de Negro* had stayed close to the Movement of Conscientious Objection in Sevilla and in 2002 joined a group called *RedPaz* (Peace Network) to set up the Peace House, *La Casa de la Paz*, with office and meeting space. Much of their work was educational, cultural, organising workshops and giving talks to women's groups, in schools, and in the community. But they also deemed 'street work' important. They were often *en la calle*, holding silent vigils, in classic WiB style, but also performing 'die-ins' and other acts of street drama. They inscribed long messages across the Plaza. There had been times they had stripped and painted their bodies with 'blood'. They retained the strongly antimilitarist stance of the *MOC* activists they had been. For example, they climbed ladders, changing the street names that honoured military men so that instead they commemorated women. They wrapped military statues in vast cloth banners. Additionally, however, *Mujeres de Negro* in Sevilla focused on sexual violence, asserting the integrity of women's bodies — a theme that women had always found difficult to address within the context of *MOC*. Bodies featured centrally in their repertoire. Sofía is a photographer and artist and used these skills to startling effect. *MdN* Sevilla's calendar for 2008 contained her photographs of their own womanly body parts with words painted on the flesh. She said, 'It is a cry, our bodies being used to shout anti-military messages. For once this is not the victimised female body. It's our bodies used on our own terms' (Cockburn 2012:42).

There was lively discussion as to whether to form a national network in Spain. At one point a nationwide *encuentro* (meeting) was called to discuss this. It attracted more than a hundred women and resulted in the founding of a state-wide body called *La Red contra las Agresiones contra las Mujeres: Mujeres de Negro* (Network against Aggression against Women: Women in Black). Each local group in the *Red* would have its own character, no formula would be imposed. They felt that, as had been demonstrated by *MOC*, an informal *asamblearismo,* structureless and fluid, was an important asset in resisting incursions and takeovers of women's initiatives by cadres of the left parties and tendencies. But they did agree to foster links across Spain and, from 1997, they established the national *encuentro* as an annual event. They also joined in the developing series of international meetings of the Network of Women's Solidarity against War, hosted by the Yugoslav women throughout the 1990s. In this way, the Sevilla women felt themselves to be part of 'a big international family'.

That family then spread from city to city across Spain, as recorded by WiB Madrid:

WOMEN IN BLACK MADRID

In 1992 the Conscientious Objectors Movement sought to identify groups or individuals in former Yugoslavia that worked against war in non-violent ways in order to support them; this is how we heard about Women in Black Belgrade. In Madrid we created the Platform for Peace in the Balkans, a network coordinating various groups, and we supported WiB Belgrade for several years by donating the portion of our taxes that would otherwise go to fund the Ministry of Defence — known as Fiscal Objection to Spanish Military Spending. Later, in 1999, we created WiB Madrid. We came from anti-militarist and Christian groups, feminists and others with no previous experience in activism.

We are feminist, pacifist and antimilitarist women. Our strategies are civil disobedience, non-cooperation and non-violent direct action. We call on citizens to take responsibility for the war policies of our country. We go to the streets in silence, wearing black as a sign of mourning for all victims of war. Two of our slogans at the monthly vigils are: 'Let's eliminate war and violence from history and from our lives' and 'Change military expenditure to social expenditure'.

We try to reflect on the characteristics of Women in Black and apply those to the challenges of everyday life. Because we are all volunteers and have other responsibilities, we try to understand our different rhythms and avoid leaving anyone behind. We are a complex group with different levels of involvement. If we want to build a more just and less violent world, we need new ways of working. The group and the relationships that are formed within it are a 'protected space' where we can test those new ways of doing and learn from mistakes.

Horizontality is one of our trademarks; we seek to decide by consensus. We take turns at doing the various activities so all of us are necessary but unessential. One of the challenges is to be in tune with each other's rhythms, motivations and commitments, given that we don't want to stop the energy of those who want to and can get more involved. Each month there is a Coordinator who invites the rest of us to fortnightly meetings, sends out the agenda, chairs the meeting and writes the minutes. The Coordinator also organises the vigil in the Plaza Mayor in Madrid at noon on the last Sunday of every month and assigns tasks (taking the banner to the vigil, distributing the press release). In additional meetings, she circulates information about the topic to be discussed, hands out meeting guidelines and writes the minutes. The previous month's Coordinator writes the press release and creates the banner with the agreed message. We aim to take care of ourselves, with food and drink to share during the meetings.

Every September we update our goals and activities. We review our results and feelings every three months, and share our opinions via email, taking care of the way that we write so that messages don't become a source of conflict. When a woman calls us and says she wants to know more about WiB or participate in our activities, we invite her to join us on the monthly vigil and send her the link to our website. One of us becomes her godmother so she receives additional information and feels more integrated.

We participate in local, national and international campaigns, frequently in partnership with other groups: EVA, campaigns against arms fairs in Madrid, Embrace of the People (*Abrazos de los Pueblos*), Opening Frontiers Caravan (*Caravana Abriendo Fronteras*), *Colectivo Noviolencia y Educación*, Amnesty International (especially AI's women's group), 8 March International Women's Day, Wool against Weapons 2014 — we knitted scarfs and a few of us joined in — and we have joined demonstrations against military bases in the UK, organised by Trident Ploughshares and WiB London [see Chapter 3].

In Israel we joined WiB campaigns with New Profile and other pacifist, conscientious objector and antimilitarist groups to oppose the occupation of Palestine. We have joined mobilisations in Colombia with the *Organización Femenina Popular*

(OFP), *Ruta Pacífica de las Mujeres* and *Comunidad de Paz de San José de Apartadó*; and we have invited their members to Spain, where we help them organise events to speak about their work. In the Balkans we have strong relations with WiB Belgrade and participate in their anniversaries, Srebrenica memorials, the Women's Tribunal in Sarajevo and other mobilisations.

We keep in touch with other groups and women through the international WiB network and *encuentros*, translating emails for the Spanish WiB list and helping to administer the email lists. Our publications include booklets on *Horizontality as one of the Trademarks of Women in Black against War* (2010) and *A Few Reflections on the characteristics of Women in Black against War* (2013). Our book on *Women who Opposed World War I* has been translated into English (La Malatesta, 2018 and 2019).

Our blog is at http://www.mujeresdenegromadrid.blog-spot.com.es/ and our webpage at Mujer Palabra http://mujer-palabra.net/activismo/mdnmadrid/. We have an email list for our monthly invitations, press releases and other documents (mdnmadrid@mujerpalabra.net).

WiB Madrid in turn inspired WiB Toledo, as Kika reports:

WOMEN IN BLACK IN TOLEDO

I got to know WiB Madrid on 1 May 2015 and felt that we needed to create a group like that in Toledo. The vigils give me lots of satisfaction because through them we have the opportunity to speak with people from other cities and have met tourists who know about WiB in other countries and also people who come from countries in conflict.

My personal experience has been very positive, and the creation of the group has been an opportunity to speak up, and campaign. It has been truly important in my life. We still have a lot of work to do and need to be more active. I truly appreciate the perseverance and effort of each of our WiB Toledo members

Women in Black Against War began in Toledo in 2015, to oppose injustice, war, militarism and other forms of violence. The last Saturday of every month, at 12:00, we stand in silent vigils in the main square in our town, wearing black, because we are in mourning for all war victims. We distribute leaflets about the chosen topic each month. During the pandemic, we posted them on social media.

Each year we participate in the Summer Antimilitarist School held in Madrid and help SOS Greece, a group that supports refugee camps in Greece, and also PROEM – AID, a not-for profit group of emergency professionals that organises rescue operations in the Mediterranean.

We are very close to WiB Madrid and we have participated in their activities and they have also joined ours. We held the most recent meeting of WiB groups in Spain in Toledo and it was a fantastic experience. Women from different cities came, we exchanged experiences and we proposed ideas to further develop our work in our cities. Internationally, we are part of the international WiB email list and several of us went to the WiB conference in South Africa in 2017.

There are now (2022) *Mujeres de Negro* groups in Barcelona, Madrid, Seville and Toledo. Yolanda Rouiller, from *Mujeres de Negro* Barcelona, created an international email list in Spanish in 1999, working with Lieve Snellings from Leuven WiB who takes care of the list in Flemish, French, Dutch and English. Both still moderate the international WiB list, sharing and translating information from WiB groups across several languages and at least 60 countries.

WiB Leuven

We shall now focus on one small spot on the world map — the city of Leuven in the Flemish-speaking part of Belgium — pursuing the theme of communication and connection in Women in Black. Belgium is a multilingual country, something that presents every Belgian with a challenge; the line that divides the northern Flemish/Dutch-speaking part of Belgium (Flanders) from the southern French-speaking part (Wallonia) runs horizontally across the country and cuts it roughly in half. There is also a small region of eastern Belgium, bordering Germany, where the official language is German. In the centrally placed capital city of Brussels, the French and Flemish languages have equal status. To this complexity we have to add that English is also widely spoken by Belgians. This linguistic proficiency may well be the reason that Women in Black in Belgium so effectively co-fostered the development of the WiB network's communication system, multilingual email lists and website.

In French, Women in Black is known as *Femmes en Noir*, in Dutch it is *Vrouwen in het Zwart*, and in German *Frauen in Schwarz*. But this several-sided Belgian WiB did not come into existence until 1994. Leading up to that moment were fifteen years of feminist antimilitarist activism in Belgium. The following account of that early part of the story draws on two papers prepared early in 2019 by WiB activists Lieve Snellings and Ria Convents, both resident in Leuven. In other ways, too, these two women have contributed greatly to this chapter. Lieve was born in 1954, in the Dutch-speaking north of Belgium, is a lesbian, and has a long career as an immensely creative feminist writer and photographer, producing work particularly for children, and about animals and nature. Totally committed to her work and activism, she says 'It's better to lose yourself in your passion than to lose your passion'. Ria, also born in Flanders in 1954, started out in life as a lawyer, working in association with a shelter for battered women. Like Lieve, she is a lesbian, and says, 'That's my *being*; my feminism is my ideological and political "choice"'.[6]

Ria and Lieve were first drawn to feminist pacifist activism by two mobilisations in consecutive years, 1980 and 1981, that took place far from Belgium. The first was the Women's Pentagon Action in the USA; the second the Greenham Common Women's Peace Camp in the UK. On 17 November 1980, 2,000 women besieged the Pentagon, headquarters of the US Department of Defence, in Arlington, near Washington DC, in an impressive action, news of which travelled fast around the world. They took with them four huge puppets and encircled the building, mourning death by placing gravestones on the grass and celebrating the web of life by weaving yarn across the entrances. It was a noisy demonstration. They chanted, shouted and banged on cans. There were many arrests: some women were shackled at wrist and ankle and incarcerated for several weeks. While these women were protesting against US militarism and militarisation, they also singled out nuclear weapons for particular attention. They focused on the Pentagon 'because it is the workplace of imperial power which threatens us all'. They wrote, 'Every day while we work, study, love, the colonels and generals who are planning our annihilation walk calmly in and out the doors of its five sides. To carry out their plans they have been making between three and six nuclear bombs every day. They have accumulated over 30,000 … We fear for the life of this planet, our Earth, and the life of our children who are our human future.'[7]

Hearing about the Women's Pentagon Action, Lieve and other Belgian feminists living in Leuven got together to form an antimilitarist women's group. They had seen these women developing a new language in which protests went hand in hand with art, ideas and emotions. They learned from them and looked for other ways to do actions so that grief and anger could find ways to express themselves constructively.

The Belgian women's second inspiration was the Women's Peace Camp at Greenham Common. Lieve, Ria and other Belgian women travelled there on several occasions to support the campers. Lieve said, 'Many of us in the Belgian movement were lesbians. Identifying yourself as a Greenham Common woman was saying you were a non-violent feminist peace activist, and you made all these links between domestic violence, homophobia, and war. Peace is possible only when everybody has basic human rights, when there is no racism, no abuse or rape of children and women, no homophobia' (Interview with Cynthia Cockburn, 2019).

The next step forward in Leuven women's activism occurred in 1983 when, in response to the rape of a woman worker at the Women's Refugee House, a group was formed called Women

Against Rape. They wrote a statement against rape and proposed some concrete actions/measures that the City authority could take/implement. They mounted a women's action. (Some men asked to join it — whereon the women proposed that they organise their own demonstration, as men, against rape.) The women for their part dressed in black and, keeping silent except for the beating of half a dozen drums, they approached the City Hall. They entered and sat in an orderly way in the public chamber, where they read out a 'letter of mourning' and their demands on the authority. As they descended the stairs on their way out, however, the police rushed in to arrest them. Undeterred, the women subsequently pursued the rape theme by attempting to bury a statue in the town — an image that they felt encouraged the abuse of women. Named 'Fiery Margriet', the sculpture represented a thirteenth-century woman, 'a proud servant girl,' who had been raped and killed. Legend had it that her body had risen up out of the river, surrounded by a bright light. The murdered Fiery Margriet was believed to perform miracles; the townspeople had built a chapel in her name. Our present-day Leuven women, however, hated this statue, as in the past drunken Leuven students had organized mass rapes near it. That is why they now set out to pull it down.

The same year, on Flemish Women's Day, 11 November 1983, these women formed a new group called AMKK (*Anti-Militaristische Koffie Klatsh* — Anti-Militarist Coffee Klatch). Their banner read, 'Every three seconds a child dies of hunger. Every three seconds 3 million Belgian francs are spent on weapons.' The AMKK later changed its name to Women Against Militarism (WAM). Once they knew that in 1985 Cruise missiles would arrive in Belgium (and that the Pope was going to visit the country that year) they planned an action in January 1985 in Leuven to paint '*ZIJ KOMT*' ('she's coming') and '*VROUWEN TEGEN MILITARISME*' (women against militarism) on public buildings. Two of the women were arrested the morning after (one of them was the mother of three young children) and held in prison for a month. A third woman was also arrested and jailed later. Solidarity demonstrations started immediately in Leuven, organised by the *Vrouwensolidariteit* (Women's solidarity) group. About 50 women managed to organise large demonstrations; members of parliament went to the prison and started discussions in parliament; events were planned to raise money to pay the legal and other costs. Later the three women in prison were sentenced to jail for the period they had already served, and fined. Leuven now knew more about the peace activists, who remained active. WAM continued many non-violent actions at a military base near Florennes, in the French-speaking part of Belgium, where US nuclear missiles were located (as they were at Greenham Common). WAM and other peace groups bought a house opposite the police station at Florennes and renovated it for use as a launch pad for actions against nuclear missiles and other aspects of militarism. One was to bring thousands of women to 'embrace the base', Greenham-style. Seventeen women were held in custody for a month for demonstrating; WAM demonstrations were held near the prison to support them.

In December 1989, Ria joined a group of ten women visiting Palestine, a year after the beginning of the (first) intifada. The group consisted of two women from the Green Party, two from the Socialist Party, two from the Communist Party, two from NGOs and two independent feminists. Ria was one of the latter and the only one to visit an Israeli women's group who were supporting Palestinian women in prison. Many women (and men) financially supported Ria to go, and afterwards the group reported on what they found in a booklet and travelled around Belgium with slides of what they had seen.

Then, fast forward to the early 1990s, when the USA began its much-disputed bombing of Iraq. Women against Militarism and others came together in a group called Women Against War. Some of them, including Ria and Lieve, travelled to an international Women's Peace Conference in Tunis in February

1991 with about 1,500 participants (including the actress and campaigner Vanessa Redgrave) and on their return, gave the Belgian prime minister a report on their findings. They called on him and his government to pressure the US administration to cease the bombing of Iraq. The next challenge of the 1990s, after Iraq, was the outbreak in 1992 of the wars that tore apart the former Yugoslavia, as we have seen. In this context, the shape and name of Belgian feminist pacifist activism changed once again, groups and individuals organising as something they called the Women's Action Collective (*Vrouwen Aktie Kollectief*, or VAK for short). VAK women forged particularly strong links with *Žene u Crnom* (WiB) in former Yugoslavia (see Chapter 2). It happened through a very energetic and effective 'aid' action developed by VAK — driving convoys of supplies along the thousand-odd miles of road from Belgium to the town of Tuzla in Bosnia-Herzegovina, to support the war-beleaguered women there. This action mirrored similar convoys from Women in Black in Italy and Women's Aid to Former Yugoslavia from the UK.

Lieve Snellings was one of the VAK women to travel with the first convoy at the end of October 1994. They travelled in a truck laden with hygiene products, cleaning materials, tights and other items requested by the women of Tuzla. The truck had two drivers, 'Moniek and Bert', Lieve recounts, and was accompanied by a car 'in which Jenny, Dimphna, Aldegonde and I travelled'. They found the women of Tuzla living in dire conditions. Water supply was reduced to a few hours a day. Electricity functioned only every second day. There was no money to pay salaries, so health and education services were minimal. While in Tuzla, Lieve made a working visit to the University Clinic of Tuzla and took down the specifications of the mammography scanner they needed — which the Leuven women managed to obtain and transport on a future convoy to Tuzla.

The VAK convoy group later managed to 'bring Tuzla back to Leuven'. Lieve tells the story this way:

In Tuzla I met Christiana Lambrinidis. She was there with a Greek women's delegation, conducting creative writing workshops in a refugee camp in Tuzla. The women were urging Christiana, 'Go and tell our stories'. Later we talked about this and VAK decided to invite Christiana to write a theatre play about it (interview with Cynthia Cockburn, 2019).

In doing so, Christiana had the idea of enriching the Tuzla testimonies with autobiographical descriptions of refugee life in exile. She met five refugee women from Sarajevo and Mostar living near Antwerp in Belgium, who were keen on this idea, and together they started a theatre project, drawing on their own experiences, enriched by the Tuzla testimonies. In that way, the refugee experience was enlarged to include two important issues. One was the particular identity of the Muslim women of Tuzla, who did not wear hijab or chador and stressed their distinctiveness as 'European' Muslims. A second was sexuality. Lieve said,

> We were happy that an 'out' lesbian was there to 'perform' the Tuzla testimonies. A more humane world for refugees is a more humane world for inhabitants, because we are all inhabitants and we all are, and women are, displaced — displaced from our inner selves.

Christiana's production took the title 'Women of Tuzla, Sarajevo and Mostar: A Mythography of Courage'. She was impressed by seeing the refugee women 'coming in contact with their own strength, a strength they had always had, and now recognized'. She saw how they came close to each other, supported and comforted each other, without losing their sense of self. Lieve photographed the rehearsals and performances of the production. She rejoiced in what she saw and heard: 'Acceptance of differences in themselves, the differences of others — it seemed so important. I was so lucky to have witnessed this mutual empowerment.' The play was performed in

1996 in the Bourla Schouwburg in Antwerp, Belgium, and also on Christiana's home ground in Athens, Greece.

Vrouwen in het Zwart: The First Decade

During their travels to Tuzla, the Leuven women had become aware of *Žene u Crnom*'s protests against the wars and 'ethnic cleansing', and in particular they learned about the 'Women in Black' vigils *ŽUC* were holding regularly in Belgrade. VAK-women Leen Vandamme and Edith Rubinstein went to the International WIB Conference in Novi Sad in Yugoslavia in the summer of 1993. They invited Sonja Prodamovic from WiB-Belgrade to the Women's Day in Belgium on 11 November 1993. Lieve says, 'As VAK we wanted to support these women too'. Ria Convents travelled several times to join the women in Belgrade, sometimes accompanied by Leen Vandamme. And gradually, Lieve says, 'we women of VAK started to feel ourselves *to be* Women in Black. And we started to organise vigils and demonstrations *as such,* in Belgium' (interview with Cynthia Cockburn, 2019).

The first Women in Black vigil to be held in Belgium, on 12 January 1994, was not in Leuven, but in the capital city, Brussels. The women chose to position it in front of the headquarters of the European Commission, since the EU was considered to be partly responsible for the continuation of the conflict in Yugoslavia. A few months later, on 2 March, the Leuven women mounted their first WiB vigil, on Wednesday, as in Belgrade, in front of Leuven's City Hall. Their intention from the start was that it would be a weekly vigil, between 12 noon and 1 p,m,, during which they would maintain silence and dress in black. Ria was a regular. Lieve came occasionally, whenever she could. Others at these early vigils included Mieke Coremans, Chris Gooris and Carla van den Bergh, accompanied by women from the shelter for battered women and some women from NGOs. The vigils continued for the duration of the wars in Yugoslavia — not only in Leuven but also in Ghent, Antwerp, Brugge,

Leper, Mechelen en Herentals and Overijse. The participants were mainly women from the women's and peace movements that had emerged in the 1980s. The meetings, networking and link-making for these vigils were mostly organised by VAK (the Women's Action Committee).

After the Oslo Agreement (which brought a temporary so-called peace between Israel and Palestine), Israeli Women in Black organised an International WiB Conference in December 1994. Ria went to this, and to all the annual WiB International Conferences held in Yugoslavia (1995 - 2001), reporting back to WiB Leuven (as well as to the press and TV there).

There was a pause in regular vigils in Leuven from the end of 1995 when the Dayton Agreement was signed, halting the fighting in Bosnia-Herzegovina. But WiB activism continued, and the women from the vigils continued to see each other every Wednesday, for lunchtime discussions. They were ready to start vigils again in 1999, with the outbreak of conflict in Kosovo (see Chapter 2), when the Belgian women (unlike their sisters in *Žene u Crnom*) were unanimous in agreeing that they must protest against NATO intervention. On this occasion, Belgian security services banned WiB vigils in two cities, Antwerp and Brussels. But elsewhere they persisted. In honour of their tireless activism, WiB Leuven were asked to open the national peace demonstrations in Belgium in 1999.

There was another pause in vigils until the US and UK started bombing Afghanistan in October 2001 (the intervention they called 'Operation Enduring Freedom') in response to the bombing of the 'twin towers' in New York on 11 September. At this point, the Leuven women wrote a statement, jointly with *Artsen voor Vrede* (Doctors for Peace), *Voor Moeder Aarde* (For Mother Earth), *Vrede* (Peace) and *Moeders voor Vrede* (Mothers for Peace), entitled 'In Solidarity with the Worldwide Victims of Violence'. And at the national demonstration against a new war with Iraq, held in Brussels on 17 November 2001, a representative of WiB Leuven gave a speech on behalf of the Belgian

Peace Movement. They held occasional vigils in cooperation with the French-speaking WiB in Brussels and ensured that their texts were in three languages: Dutch, French and English. Just after the start of the new millennium, Leuven *Vrouen in het Zwart* turned more of their attention to the oppression of Palestinians. Lieve says, 'We felt compelled to show our solidarity with Palestinians, and with their Israeli supporters, in calling for a just peace'. First and foremost, the Occupation had to end. When the Women's Coalition for Peace sent out a call for actions worldwide for 2 June 2002, the thirty-fifth anniversary of the Occupation of Palestine, and joined the campaign for 'BDS' (Boycott, Divestment, and Sanctions of Israeli products), a response was organised by the Belgian Action Platform Palestina, a cooperation between different peace and women's groups, trade unions and NGOs, in the Flemish north and French-speaking south of Belgium. Women in Black took part in this action in twenty-three cities across the Flemish part of Belgium.

2002 was an important year for Women in Black in Leuven. It marked a new start, and since then they have been continuously on the street in a weekly Wednesday midday vigil at the entrance of Leuven City Hall. On 11 November 2002 Leuven women organised an event for Belgian Women's Day on the theme of 'violence, and violence against women'. Three international guests came and spoke on this occasion: Edna Zaretsky from Israel, Jihan Anastas from Bethlehem in Palestine and Sonja Prodamovic from WIB-Belgrade. Speaking at a celebration conducted at the monument of the 'Unknown War-Woman', they embraced each other and declared 'Whatever our leaders say or do, we refuse to be enemies. The use of weapons must stop, they have never solved any problem and have only brought more misery.' The Leuven women reminded their public of the United Nations Security Council Resolution 1325, passed just two years previously, which advocated 'the involvement of women in all of the implementation mechanisms of conflict resolution'. In response to the often-heard doubt, 'what does it matter what WE do?', Anastas responded:

> Your actions bring direct pressure on our governments. Of equal importance, your actions provide us with connections, and a sense that we aren't standing alone in our struggles … That solidarity gives us the strength to resist all forms of discrimination — all of them insane, many barbaric — including ethnic cleansing, militarism and the killing fields mentality, and of course gender-based violence, sexism and homophobia in Bethlehem we say: as long as one person is still searching, nothing is totally lost. And we are searching for peace with many (Cynthia Cockburn interview with Lieve, 2019).

At a well-attended panel with Edna Zaretsky, Jihan Anastas and Sonja Prodamovic, Mieke Coremans of Leuven WiB called for the renewal of Women in Black weekly vigils. And two days later, on 13 November 2002, they began again. The vigils inspired other kinds of activism, too. Leuven women attended the international Women in Black conference in 2003 in Marina di Masso in Italy, the 2005 conference in Jerusalem, and the 2007 conference in Valencia. Some of them went to the Faslane nuclear submarine base in Scotland in October 2006 to join the British women's actions against the UK's nuclear weapons. They sent representatives to conferences in Bogotá in 2011, Montevideo in 2013, Bangalore in 2015 and Cape Town in 2018. They made sure to contribute funding to enable WiB from poorer countries to attend these events.

Europe-wide encuentro

It was the women of the Spanish *Mujeres de Negro* who, in 2012, had the idea of organising the first Europe-wide WiB *encuentro* (as opposed to a fully international conference), hoping that with the lesser distances and lower travel costs, more women would be drawn to attend. It took place in Sevilla. The idea was picked up and carried forward by *Vrouwen in het Zwart* of Leuven, who organised the second European *encuentro* over three days in early May 2014, to coincide with the centenary of the destruction of Leuven in World War 1. They chose as the title of the *encuentro* the words of Indian feminist author Arundhati Roy: 'Hear the new world breathing ... she is coming!' Around 100 women attended, from more than twenty countries. The conference explored issues currently critical for Europe, including the crises in Ukraine, Israel's continuing occupation of Palestine, the international arms trade, and European military interventions in countries such as Afghanistan, Iraq, Syria, Libya, DR Congo and Mali. Discussions covered the expansion of NATO; implementation of UN Security Council Resolution 1325; the boycott campaign against Israel; and feminist activism against nuclear weapons in Europe.

Lepa Mladjenovic from Belgrade was present and contributed to a discussion of lesbianism in the peace movement. Interestingly, the conversation referred back to a visit she had made to Belgium thirteen years previously, when she had been a guest speaker at a 'Lesbian Day' event. Lieve recalled how Lepa had then credited the Belgian women with being an inspiration to the nascent and cautious lesbianism of the era of the convoys to Tuzla, described earlier. Lepa told the Leuven women, 'During the war so many lesbians and gays came with solidarity convoys to former Yugoslavia, but no one was out. We just couldn't do this! But it would have been SO important for us.' She said of herself, 'I was one of these lesbians who didn't say, "I'm a lesbian" - even when a woman asked me why I wasn't married. Why? I had nothing to lose! Was I afraid they wouldn't like me anymore if they knew?' Lieve said, 'Lepa's words were very confronting. I understood very clearly how important it was to be out, especially in war zones and when you are supporting the peace movement.'[8]

Many of those who attended this event from other European countries felt that the idea of a European *encuentro* was something worth sustaining. It had given European WiB a sense of what was distinctive about the issues of peace and war in Europe, of the role European countries played in provoking and preventing conflicts, and of the need for a conscious, growing and changing feminist antimilitarism in Europe.

Then, on 2 March 2019, the Leuven women marked twenty-five years of Women in Black with a day of activities. The celebration was attended by 150 women, including fifteen from other countries. From London, Liz Khan, Rebecca Johnson and Heena Thompson travelled there, and met up not only with the Belgian women but visitors from Bosnia-Herzegovina, France, Serbia, Croatia, Spain, Israel, Austria and Armenia. They brought the programme back and told London WiB the latest news from this Leuven group. *Vrouwen en het Zwart* held an 'academic session' with several speakers, Belgian and others, inside the City Hall, and then, between 3 and 4 p.m., at their customary site in front of the City Hall, mounted a special vigil, in which they were joined not only by their WiB guests but also by other peace activists from the town. They had prevailed on the Carillonneur of Leuven to play some peace peals on the church bells during the vigil. Then from six till eight in the evening all and sundry were invited to a grand reception by Leuven's city authority.[9]

Later in the same year, a celebration of lesbian feminists in the peace movement was held at Leuven City Hall, and remembered in a speech by Lepa Mladjenovic and Laurence Hovde celebrating Women in Black Leuven's 25th anniversary (text of the speech provided by Lepa Mladjenovic to Cynthia Cockburn in 2019):

Recognising, accepting, celebrating lesbian feminists in the peace movement

On 12.12 in 2012 at 12 o'clock in this City Hall of Leuven there was a wonderful lesbian marriage event with Nans Lutyens and Ria Convents, the moderator of today's historic event. I believe many activists here remember this celebration of love.

We lesbian feminist peace activists have a very deep experience of what is a heterosexual patriarchal world, that has pressured us from our childhood with a heterosexual world vision and life values. In the meantime, we also learned that neo-capitalism is manufacturing heterosexuality as the norm and compulsory regime; we had to invest our energy and wisdom to transform it in our diverse lesbian community loves.

Over the last hundred years of the women's peace movement, there have always been women active in the peace movement who have had to hide their lesbian identity. Many of us were searching for radical movements where we could be out loud lesbians and be disobedient. So, 25 years ago, we lesbian feminist peace activists insisted that we be recognised as lesbians in the WOMEN IN BLACK MOVEMENT. AND WE WERE. We found a space of sisterhood and solidarity in WOMEN IN BLACK.

OUR JOURNEY OF ALLIANCES started at WOMEN IN BLACK meetings in Jerusalem and Novi Sad back in 1993. We were continuing the courageous practice of visibility of lesbians in the GREENHAM COMMON anti-nuclear women's movement in UK. Every Women in Black meeting from then on has had a discussion or workshop on lesbians in the anti-war movement. Leuven Women in Black has fantastic lesbian feminist peace activists — we are proud of their visible lesbian activism within the peace activism in Belgium.

We lesbian feminists are contributing to the revolutionary spaces we create together, with a clear statement that the ethics of peace we desire recognises differences among people, as well as lesbian existence.

From the beginnings of Women in Black, out lesbians linked activism for peace and justice with working against sexual discrimination and male violence against women. In the past 25 years, we have made many successes in the visibility of lesbians, but discrimination, racism, lesbophobia and violence continue to be used to silence lesbian love in many places. That is why we two stand here in front of you to say: The more different we are in the movement, the more power we have. Lesbian feminists bring to the movement the love between women in a way not seen in history before we arrived. Love is peace. Love is justice. Love is power!

A communications system for Women in Black

Let us leave the history of *Vrouwen in het Zwart* at that celebratory moment, and turn back to the development of WiB communications, in which WiB Leuven played a key part. At the end of the 1980s, when Women in Black first started, a commercial internet service was imminent but scarcely yet a reality. It was not until the mid-1990s, in the context of the wars in former Yugoslavia, that the internet began to have a significant impact on WiB communication. A project initiated by War Resisters International had set up *zamir.net* ('for peace'), as mentioned in Chapter 2, providing internet for *ŽuC*, the women's centre in Zagreb, and a host of other anti-war and aid/humanitarian NGOs. Through this network, women in Leuven, Italy and the UK were able to contact women in Yugoslavia to arrange aid convoys. However, during early WiB activities there was little attempt to develop a 'communication strategy'. Country groups communicated within themselves more than with each other. An international WiB email list first came into existence in 1998, moderated by Yolanda Rouiller, a Spanish WiB. She managed one in the English language and one in Spanish, translating from one to the other.

At the international WiB *encuentro* in Marina di Massa, Italy, in August 2003, a hope had been expressed that Women in Black would continue to enjoy the advantages of spontaneity and diversity, while avoiding bureaucratisation and centralisation. At the same time, WiB wanted to increase effectiveness as a worldwide activist network. It was strongly felt that WiB ought to develop an intelligent and democratic use of the internet. Some eighteen volunteers put their names forward to comprise an international working group; a month later, an unmoderated group mailing list was established. The group, which was open to any WiB activist, sought to ensure representation from a range of regions, especially some that were located in the 'founding' regions — Israel/Palestine, Italy and former Yugoslavia — and the global south.

In the summer of 2003, three email accounts were established — English, Spanish and French. At that point, Lieve Snellings in Belgium, who was fluent in Flemish and English, became its attentive and hard-working coordinator as she continues to be to the present day. Next, a French language list was initiated, and a little later, an Italian language list was created by Marianita di Ambrogio, fluent in Italian, French and Spanish. Yolanda Rouiller, a Spanish WiB, took on the Spanish-speaking list. Of course, many, if not all, 'national' WiB groups continue to have their own internal e-lists. The principle that the subscribers to each of the language lists would operate as a self-governing information 'community' was quickly established, through the intervention of the moderators, who made decisions about the conduct of their own list, and their list alone. The language lists operated only in 'mailing-out' mode, for simplicity.

After some months operating these parallel lists, however, it became clear that a discussion forum was needed, and 'the interactive list' was established. In theory, communication on the interactive list might be in any language, relying on volunteers to translate as appropriate. In practice it was conducted almost exclusively in English.

By the time of the Jerusalem conference in 2005, there was an international Women in Black website (www.womeninblack.org), initially supported by funds from the Coalition of Women for a Just Peace in Israel. The website had pages describing Women in Black; summarising its history; listing vigils worldwide, country by country and town by town; and a page on 'how to start your own vigil', together with a form on which new vigils might send details, to be added to the list. The usual facilities existed for updating the site with announcement of events and actions, creating links to related sites, and attaching documents. It was decided that newcomers wishing to subscribe first submit their personal details and receive no objections to their doing so.

In the more recent period (2011-21) the several email lists have continued to be functional and busy, each in the caring hands of its moderator. After the international conference in Valencia in 2007, grant funding was raised to establish a new and better website. The aim was to give each group its own portal through which they would be able to change and update their own material, without the need for technical help. Sixty Women in Black groups are now represented on the site www.womeninblack. org, sharing information, actions, photos and ideas for moving forward from the patriarchal culture of war and violence against women, towards a feminist vision for peace.

NOTES

1   The principal sources for this part of the chapter are the internal publications and website of the Movimiento de Objección de Conciencia (MOC), later renamed Alternativa Antimilitarista (AA-MOC), and interviews by Cynthia Cockburn with a number of its members during 2008.
2   Duda Petrovic, Gordana Radic, Jadranka Milicevic, Jasmina Arsova, Sonja Prodanovic, Staša Zajović, Rada Zarkovic and Violeta Djikanovic (ŽuC 1944:149).
3   The situation was complicated by the admission of women to the armed forces in 1988. Anti-militarist feminists in MOC were obliged to distance themselves from those feminists who welcomed the move on 'equality' grounds. There was nothing to be gained in their

view by women acceding to the masculinist cultural model the army represented, voluntarily signing up to a 'school of blind obedience, submission, exploitation and machismo'. (Braunw et al 1984:14)

4   From a typescript paper titled *Memoria*, written in 2007, gathered in the course of Cynthia Cockburn's research, in which some of the women recalled the history of *Mujeres de Negro* in Sevilla (Cockburn 2012:98).

5   The two papers on which this Chapter draws, and frequently quotes, in the account of the origin and development of Women in Black activism in Belgium are unpublished and were supplied specifically for the purposes of writing this chapter. Ria Convents' paper is titled '*Vrouwen in het Zwart: Tegen Oorlog in Geweld – Femmes en Noir: Contre la Guerre et la Violence*: History of the Worldwide Women in Black Movement', while that of Lieve Snellings is 'Deeper Herstory of WiB Leuven (and a Bit About the Flemish part of Belgium)'.

6   From 'Unity Statement of the Women's Pentagon Action, November 1980', on the website www.wloe.org/WLOE-en/background/wpastatem. html (accessed June 2021)

7   As a result of their organising this European *encuentro*, Pax Christi Flanders nominated *Vrouwen in het Zwart, Leuven,* an 'ambassador of peace'.

8   The women who at this moment constituted the Leuven WiB group, and together who issued this invitation to the 25th anniversary celebration, were Nani Sneyers, Marianne van de Goorberg, Ria Convents, Carla van den Bergh, Chris Gooris, Mieke de Vreede, Mieke Coremans, Dory Pelgrims, Rita Vangool, and Maria Vandoren.

CHAPTER 5

JUSTICE FOR WOMEN: FROM INDIA TO SOUTH AFRICA

India saw one of the earliest expressions of Women in Black, after Corinne Kumar connected with Gila Svirsky (WiB in Israel Palestine) at a seminar in California in 1992. Corinne, who had founded an organisation called CIEDS (Centre for Informal Education and Development Studies) in Bangalore in 1975, came back from the US burning to introduce the idea of women standing in black to protest against violence to India. CIEDS was a mixed organisation that campaigned for social justice and equality. But the women soon took a theoretical turn away from the organisation, setting more store by local and individual experiences and creativity — and developing an articulate critique of patriarchy.

In 1979, Donna Fernandes and other women activists like Corinne decided they wanted to create distinctive spaces within CIEDS and more widely in the public arena for women to contest patriarchal violence. One of the first they brought into being was *Vimochana* — meaning 'liberation'. It was an all-women collective, opposing violence in all its forms — that of imperialism, of militarism and war, and communal violence between Hindu and Muslim extremists. Gender was a thread running through all their analyses. They represented the pursuit of weapons supremacy by the Indian state as 'macho posturing' and described the fascist *Hindutva* movement as 'hyper-masculinised'. One of their slogans was 'Violence-free homes make violence-free communities. Violence-free communities make a violence-free world.' *Vimochana* gave birth to a number of sister organisations, all under the rubric of CIEDS, that included a women's crisis centre for women escaping violence *(Angala)*, a women's shelter *(Kuteera)*, housing fifty women and a staff of six or seven, a women's bookshop *(Streelekha)*, a vocational training project for women (in motor vehicle maintenance) and nationwide campaigns on such matters as the sexual selection of female foetuses for abortion, the prostitution of women and the many unnatural deaths of women in marriage. How did they become Women in Black?

WiB travels to Bangalore

Corinne attended one of *Žene u Crnom's* annual conferences in Novi Sad, after she came back from meeting Gila Svirsky in 1992. Struck by the effectiveness of WiB activism and vigils, she carried the practice back to Bangalore, where she believed it could be a good strategy for *Vimochana* to 'take things to the public'. This makes them one of the oldest groups in the movement, preceded only by Israel Palestine, Italy, former Yugoslavia and the UK. The first WiB vigil in India was mounted in the aftermath of the surge of violence related to Hindu extremists' destruction of an ancient Muslim holy place, the Babri Masjid Mosque, in 1993. For a time, they repeated the vigils weekly, on a Thursday, in Bangalore's Cubbon Park. Mostly they followed the WiB formula of stillness, blackness and silence. But sometimes the women would take more dramatic action in the streets, for instance parading cut-out images to represent women victims of dowry killings.

While on a research visit to *Vimochana* in 2004-5, Cynthia Cockburn attended one of their vigils. She remembered standing on the steps of the city hall in Bangalore as the daylight faded, the parakeets and black kites circled overhead, and the crowds returned from work. On that occasion, the women's bold black signs, with white lettering, addressed the recurrent communal violence in the region between Hindus and Muslims. During her visit she had long conversations with Madhu Bhusan and other women of *Vimochana* and learned that there had been a good deal of continuity and cohesion over the previous twenty years. The core group had been almost the same women since the mid-1980s. They came from Hindu, Muslim, Christian and other backgrounds and spoke six languages between them, but they identified less with these cultures of origin than with a shared secularism and feminism. Madhu told Cynthia:

> People tend to see us as women of no faith, with no husbands and no children. In reality most of us are married — although some are single, divorced or in relationships. But in our work we challenge accepted norms and family values. People can't believe that a woman could have a husband and be able to run around as we do.[1]

The key issue for *Vimochana* was the multiple manifestations of violence against women endemic in Indian society. Their leaflets describe the perennial violence on the national scale: the violence of imperialism (often in the shape of the incursions of Western capitalist enterprises into the Indian economy); of militarism and war (especially in relation to India's nuclear stand-off with Pakistan); and of communal violence, particularly between Hindus and Muslims, but also expressed in the maltreatment of untouchables (*dalits*) and tribal peoples (*adivasis*). They recognised the patriarchal-ism, the masculinism, at the heart of all of these. However, *Vimochana* were particularly galvanised by the violence visited on individual women. This included rape, and the trafficking of women into prostitution; the many unexplained deaths of married women (an average of three a day reported in Bangalore alone) that are often murders or suicides on account of dowry disputes; of violence in the name of mascu-line honour, as in disfiguring women by throwing acid; and burning women alive as witches.

Vimochana's analysis of all these kinds of violence located them not in 'tradition' but in modernity, in the context (as one of their leaflets put it) of an ever-more 'consumerist, aggressive, macho and intolerant society'. They looked on violence as a continuum, to be contested at every point. Madhu said, 'We didn't start as women against war, but as women against violence against women. Through that we came to take a stand against violence in the wider society' (Cockburn 2007:215).

Women in Black in a context of justice: the Courts of Women

Women in Black flourished in India, soon spreading from Bangalore to Madurai, Delhi, Kerala and other centres. The distinctive thing about WiB in this context was that it became deeply associated with the matter of *justice* — justice for women, redress for the wrongs inflicted on them. The *Vimochana* experience led Corinne Kumar to create a framework she called the 'Asian Women's Human Rights Council' (AWHRC). One of its core programmes was the series of events developed by Corinne called 'the Courts of Women'. A 'Court' involves an activity of two or three days, simulating a 'hearing' in front of 'judges', in which a succession of women make their cases against violence, present evidence, call witnesses and seek justice. Unlike a real court in the state's juridical system, it does not involve a prosecution and defence. The witnesses are not cross-examined, they are believed. The jury, composed of women chosen for their wisdom and experience, does not find guilt or innocence but rather listens, understands and reflects on what it hears. In Corinne's words:

> While the Courts of Women listen to the voices of the victims/survivors, they also listen to the voices of women who resist, who rebel, who refuse to turn against their dreams. They hear the voices of women from the women's and human rights movements; they hear of survival in the dailiness of life; they hear of women and

movements resisting violence in their myriad forms — war, ethnicity, fundamentalism; they hear of women struggling for work, wages, their rights to the land; they hear of how they survive — of their knowledges, their wisdoms that have been inaudible, invisible. They hear challenges to the dominant human rights discourse, whose frames have excluded the knowledges of women. The Courts of Women hear of the need to extend the discourse to include the meanings and symbols and perspectives of women. It speaks of a new generation of women's human rights. (Kumar 2015)

Beginning in late 1993, Corinne has held an impressive number of such theatrical Courts around the world. The first was in Lahore, Pakistan. By 2021 there had been forty, in Africa, the Americas, the Asia Pacific region and the Mediterranean. ii *El Taller International,* an NGO based in Tunisia, likewise founded by Corinne, carried the Courts to many other countries.

The Courts of Women seek to weave together the objective reality (through analyses of the issues) with the subjective testimonies of the women; the personal with the political; the logical with the lyrical (through video testimonies, artistic images and poetry) urging us to discern fresh insights, offering us other ways to know, inviting us to seek deeper layers of knowledge; towards creating a new knowledge paradigm. The Courts of Women are public hearings: the Court is used in a symbolic way. In the Courts, the voices of the victims/survivors are listened to. Women bring their personal testimonies of violence to the Court: the Courts are sacred spaces where women, speaking in a language of suffering, name the crimes, seeking redress, even reparation. (Corinne Kumar in an unpublished leaflet quoted in Cockburn 2007:169)

The Courts often include a Women in Black vigil — and in this way WiB surfaced in many new countries. The largest ever WiB vigil, with an estimated 30,000 participants, was also initiated by Corinne: at Beijing in 1995, at the United Nations Fourth World Conference of Women.

On one occasion, the relationship between the Courts of Women and Women in Black was reversed. Instead of a WiB vigil being attached to a Court, a Court was attached to a WiB conference. This came about in 2015, twenty-three years after *Vimochana*'s first Women in Black vigil, at Women in Black's sixteenth annual international conference. Since the conference, at the invitation of *Vimochana* and the AWHRC, was held in Bangalore, it naturally enough included a Court of Women, attended by over a thousand people.

Corinne opened the Court by inviting everyone to 're-imagine justice':

> We must speak too of *another notion of justice*; of a jurisprudence, which bringing individual and collective justice and reparation will also be transformatory for all. A jurisprudence that is able to *contextualize* and *historicize* the crimes, moving away from a justice with punishment, a justice of revenge, a *retributive justice*, to a justice seeking redress, even reparation; a justice with truth and reconciliation, a *restorative justice*, a *justice with healing*, healing individuals and communities. Can the tears and narratives of the women, these *sites of pain,* and these sites of devastation and destitution lead us to re-thinking and *re-imagining another way to justice*? What ideas and sensibilities do we need to explore and to expand the imagination of justice? Refusing to separate the affective from the rational (juridical) creates a space in which emotive demands are allowed to be voiced and collective trauma is understood. This can be a step towards re-imagining this jurisprudence from within civil society in which we are able to creatively connect

and deepen our collective insights and understanding of the *context* in which the *text* of our everyday realities is being written.

Our imaginaries must be different: The new imaginary cannot have its moorings in the dominant discourse but must seek to locate itself in a *discourse of dissent* that comes from a deep critique of the different forms of domination and violence in our times: any new imaginary cannot be tied to the dominant discourse and systems of violence and exclusion:

Perhaps, it is in the expressions of *resistance* seeking legitimacy not by the dominant standards, not from a dominant paradigm of jurisprudence, not by the rule of law, that begin to draw the contours of a new political imaginary: the Truth Commissions, the Public Hearings, the Peoples' Tribunals, the Courts of Women are expressions of a new imaginary refusing that human rights be defined and confined by the dominant hegemonic paradigm. (Corinne Kumar, Summary Report from the World Court of Women Against War, For Peace, and XVI Biennial Women in Black Conference, 15–19 November 2015, Bangalore, India)

Women at the World Court testified one by one to the violence they had experienced — Eman from Iraq, Beni from Congo, Tasneem from Kashmir, Anandi from Sri Lanka, Mejra from Bosnia, Marcelina from Uganda, Vicky from the Philippines, Faika from South Africa, Heela from Afghanistan, and many more.

Eman Khammas, speaking about the 2003 Iraq War, said it was built on three lies: 1. Iraq had weapons of mass destruction; 2. Iraq helped terrorism flourish; 3. Iraq was ruled by a dictator, and there was no democratic structure of governing. Thousands of Iraqis lost their jobs, houses and everything related to their former ways of life; Syria and Iraq, she said, were being emptied of their people and professionals, losing their valuable human resources and being occupied by militias and foreign troops and nationals. And in the last decade, four million Iraqis had become Internationally Displaced Persons (IDPs) and eight million were in urgent need of humanitarian aid.

Beni Chugh spoke of the brutal war unleashed in Congo for Tantalum, one of the most valuable and sought-after rare metals of our times, with women becoming the collateral damage in this war of economicide; wars are waged to wrest control over the country's natural resources. She said: 'In DRC forty thousand women are raped each year. Four-fifths of the population has been displaced at least once in what began as attempts at ethnic genocide in the aftermath of the Rwandan genocide. Congo's immense wealth of natural resources has always been its curse. Their first and only democratically elected head was assassinated for economic reasons. In what is acknowledged as the bloodiest war since the Second World War, the war was fought for Tantalum. Tantalum is essential to manufacture mobile telephones and laptops and therefore we all have Congolese blood on our hands. It was a lucrative war fought over natural resources, but the expense was fifty-five million Congolese and we are all guilty of abetting it.' (Corinne Kumar, Summary Report from the World Court of Women Against War, For Peace, and XVI Biennial Women in Black Conference, 15–19 November 2015, Bangalore, India).

Tasneem Akhtar from Kashmir, and Anandi Sasitharan from Sri Lanka, spoke of the trauma of internal wars sponsored and conducted by nation states. Kashmir, once an island of secularism, is now consumed by military hatred. Kashmir is a shattered valley witnessing disappearances, rape, torture, death, execution, old people whose sons have died, grief-stricken young widows and children, thousands living in refugee camps in their own homelands and countless children living in orphanages. Indicting the Indian state for the thousands of uneducated who are forced to join the cause of Jihad, she said

Kashmiri youth are affected by psychological disorders, depression, anxiety, post-traumatic stress disorders, substance abuse, suicide, drug abuse and alcoholism.

Anandi spoke of the many undisclosed torture/detention centres in Sri Lanka, where girls were kept and raped by the guards. The war in Sri Lanka was a well-planned, orchestrated genocide which the people of the country have been unable to come to terms with, as it continues in many different ways. The Sri Lankan Tamils were being treated as minorities and bombs banned by international law used against them. Many people had been displaced and their properties snatched. Because of the geo-political importance of Sri Lanka, the perpetrators are protected by the international community.

Mejra from Bosnia spoke of losing both her children to the war of ethnic cleansing by the Serbs, but she was determined not to despair: 'My son Edwin was born in 1965, and my daughter in 1969. On 14 June 1992 she and my son along with 200 young men were arrested by the militia and sent to Omarska concentration camp. When the war broke out and the last bus was leaving for Prijedor, I pleaded with them not to get involved in this cruel war. But they refused. Edna wanted to become a model; instead, she became a pile of bones with a bullet hole through her head. I searched for my children all over Bosnia. On 20 June, I found Edwin from among the 140 skeletons exhumed from the Kemljani mass grave. I recognised Edwin by his teeth. And it was very clear from the remains of Edna's clothes that she was killed by a bullet in her head. I found my children after eight years of searching, during which the whole of me was dedicated to searching for the missing — disappeared persons. Even after I found my children and buried them with dignity, I continue my mission with greater conviction. I want to see that no mother gives herself to despair' (Corinne Kumar, Summary Report from the World Court of Women Against War, For Peace, and XVI Biennial Women in Black Conference, 15–19 November 2015, Bangalore, India).

Then members of the jury spoke. One of the jurors was Rebecca Johnson, from London WiB. She later wrote,

> Lives that had seemed distant came close as listeners grappled with our own relative privileges and responsibilities … We listened to testimonies about everyday violence in poor communities living on the margins of society, where girls and women are routinely sold, bought, violated and murdered …
>
> As one of the jurors, I sat on the platform making notes on everything I heard. So many appalling, unbearable testimonies. I didn't allow myself to look away, but often found that I had covered my mouth, holding my breath …
>
> Giving the jury's response to the evidence and arguments that we had heard on that long day in Bangalore, we first paid tribute to all the witnesses — the brave, brilliant, indomitable spirit of women …
>
> The jury recalled the capitalist, colonial and patriarchal roots of the pervasive 'wars against women' and called on all — individually and collectively — to do whatever we could in our own lives to support each other, work beyond borders, expose the perpetrators of violence against women, and build peaceful, just alternatives with whatever resources we can bring together. (Johnson 2016)

The Court of Women in Bangalore 2015 concluded the conference with: '*the best way to bring justice to those who've testified … about so much loss is for us together to build a powerful global women's movement to transform this world.*'

The summary report from the Court of Women added:

> The World Courts of Women have helped to restore the voices of women who were silenced, or who have had their voices stolen by violence, poverty, oppression and denial of their human rights.

What has given us hope here today are the stories of sisterhood, solidarity, the growing power of global networks of people working nonviolently for fundamental justice and change, with women taking more and more leadership and responsibility.

Just as individual, global and structural violence, conflict and genocide were woven through the testimonies we heard, so are responsibility and transformation.

The Bangalore Court was attended by fifty Women in Black conference delegates from India and a further seventy from twenty-five other countries: Afghanistan, Algeria, Armenia, the Basque country, Belgium, Cyprus, France, Germany, India, Iran, Iraq, Israel, Italy, Kashmir, Morocco, Nepal, Netherlands, Palestine, Spain, South Africa, Sri Lanka, Sweden, Tunisia, the UK and US. More women from India were able to attend the conference than ever before and brought a unique fusion of resistance to the violence experienced by women through rape, caste discrimination, dowry murder — and through economic globalisation and the far-right backlash against women in India.

Workshops reflected the ways in which WiB actions in different countries had grown and developed in the last decades, exploring feminist alternatives to military action, genocide in Armenia; injustice, inequality and violence against women in Afghanistan; flashpoints of war — in Armenia, Palestine, North East India, Kashmir and Sri Lanka; hate politics; the culture of violence and the violence of culture; virtual gender violence — cyber-crimes against women; climate change and war; nuclear weapons and nuclear energy; mediation beyond borders; feminist antimilitarism and everyday life; lesbians and transgender in the peace and justice movement; and dancing for peace.

Some of the key issues that were discussed in each of these workshops are summarised below:

The theme of a war against women ran through many of the workshops. Afghan women spoke about worsening injustice, inequality and violence against women. Women lived in a state of terror before and after the US invasion in 2001 — and still do. [Since then the sudden withdrawal of US/UK troops and the Taliban seizure of control has of course led to an even worse situation in Afghanistan]. The ongoing contentious issue of border wars with Azerbaijan was important for Armenian WiB, but there was also a war against women. However, the younger generation of women were questioning this oppressive culture and attempting to create spaces for women to be free.

Violence against women was not only a direct consequence of state violence but also the internalisation of that violence, the *Flashpoints of war in Kashmir* workshop found. Tracing the current situation in Kashmir back to the Partition of India in 1947, women had been victims of rape at the hands of the army and paramilitary forces — crimes committed with impunity. Naga women said that what marked out North-east India from other states was the draconian Armed Forces Special Powers Act, which gives impunity to the military when they rape and murder women. While they continue to struggle to repeal the act, they had been successful in becoming integral to the peace processes of negotiations and agreements between the militant groups and the Indian Government.

Nonviolent resistance was also a theme of the *Flashpoints of war in Palestine* workshop, which looked at the barriers to Palestinians working with Israeli peace activists, in the absence of equality. In the occupied territories, settlements were expanding and Palestinian lands shrinking. Palestinians were harassed at checkpoints. Women in Black Israel said they needed to work on recognising and accepting each other's pain, and on education, truth and healing, citizenship and equal rights. The group reaffirmed that nonviolent resistance was the only solution to war, and the only way to build a culture of peace.

The *Exploring feminist alternatives to militarism* workshop reflected on how Kurdish women who are part of armed women's units in Syria and Iraq could be part of an antimilitary movement like Women in Black. Kurdish women had been at the forefront of rescuing Yazidi and other minority women who had been captured, enslaved and raped or forced into marriage by ISIS. Forty million Kurdish people were split between Iraq, Iran, Syria and Turkey when the borders between them were drawn at the end of the First World War, and they remain an oppressed minority in each country. The Kurdish Women's Movement, developed over the last two decades as part of the Kurdish national liberation struggle, had raised women's voices to the forefront in defending women against oppression and discrimination. Kurdish women had played a key role in holding back *Daesh* (ISIS), for example, in the semi-autonomous north-east province of Syria — Rojava.

The social contract in Rojava (the region's constitutional document) guarantees equality in all walks of public and private life, with a legally binding co-chairing system in political and social bodies — always one woman and one man. The Kurdish People's Protection Units in Rojava include women-only units who were at the forefront of rescuing Yazidi and other minority women who had been captured and enslaved by *Daesh* in 2014.

> According to Iraqi MP Vian Dakhil, herself a Yazidi from Sinjar, an estimated 6,383 Yazidis — mostly women and children — were enslaved and transported to ISIS prisons, military training camps, and the homes of fighters across eastern Syria and western Iraq, where they were raped, beaten, sold, and locked away.[4]

Daesh controlled huge swathes of Syria and Iraq at that time, and treated women as war bounty — to rape, murder, sell or force into marriage. Women in those areas were not allowed to go to school, work, or go out without a male relative.

The workshop brought together Women in Black from around the world to look at these complex and rapidly changing issues. Everyone taking part agreed that it was important to look at the root causes — borders drawn on a map by European powers (for example, around Israel/Palestine, Afghanistan, Syria, Iran, Iraq, Turkey) have created unstable regions and oppressed peoples. *Daesh* grew in response to US/NATO military action in Iraq, Libya and Afghanistan. They are just one of many fundamentalist armies reacting against economic and globalisation policies that are the roots of violence.

Women at the workshop did not see violence as the solution, but felt it was not up to them to judge women — like the Kurdish fighters — who take up arms to defend themselves and other women. Women in Black, as an antimilitarist movement, could support the struggle of the Kurdish women by sharing information, and showing solidarity. Women in Black campaign against organised state violence — that's where it begins, and where violence needs to end. Militarism goes hand in hand with patriarchy. The WiB conference in Bangalore was an opportunity for women from various struggles across the world to find common approaches to resist the continuum of violence against women.

The *Workshop on Climate Change and War* focused on the key arguments of Rosalie Bertell,5 who linked militarisation to climate destabilisation, connecting the many facets of the abuse of the earth to the military: toxic bases, nuclear testing, huge consumption of fossil fuel, the diversion of research funding that should be directed towards sustainability, the development of toxic chemicals like Agent Orange, which then get repackaged as commercial agricultural pesticides. Participants felt that military systems and militarisation are perhaps the greatest contributors to climate destabilisation.

The *Feminist approaches to Ban Nuclear Weapons* workshop explored connections between nuclear energy and nuclear weapons. Participants exploded the myth that nuclear energy is cheap, clean and safe; in reality, it is highly toxic due to the process of mining uranium and waste disposal. And in this so-called peaceful nuclear energy cycle, many indigenous communities have found themselves dispossessed and poisoned, the toxic legacy affecting generations; nuclear weapons are the outcomes of these nuclear energy processes. International humanitarian laws to eliminate weapons and lobby countries that do not possess nuclear weapons are key to getting them banned. It was agreed that it was necessary to explore non-nuclear options for producing energy from local and renewable energy sources like wind and water that are safe and clean.

The *Workshop on Lesbians in the Peace and Justice Movements* began with a few questions

- How do you identify in terms of gender and sexual identity?
- Tell one short story — an example what it is like to be lesbian in your world, in your family and political work?
- What was your response if you have met or worked with someone LGBTIQ?
- How can we be allies?
- What are the strengths you get from your sexual identity?

The participants identified as being women, lesbian, gender fluid, queer and bi-sexual, and discussed narratives of pain, brutal violence and resistance. There was also discussion about the ways intersectionality made the experiences of oppression and exclusion more pronounced. For example, the intersectionality of Dalits faced particular oppression.

Participants emphasised the fact that we need to work together and build allies as we struggle against an unjust world. Our struggle should not be limited to LGBTIQ issues. As Audre Lorde said, there is no such thing as a single-issue struggle, because we don't lead single-issue lives. The group felt that binaries crept into and arrested the struggle to get acceptance and tolerance and deliberated on the strengths and positive emotions associated with sexual and gender identity, such as the ability to empathise with varied oppressions; growing self-esteem leading to greater solidarity, pride and community belonging; freedom of expression; social activism and advocacy and the greater inclination to demand social justice.

Conference participants were also invited to visit the women's shelter run by *Vimochana* (the same collective as Women in Black) in the countryside just outside of Bangalore, and were amazed by the beautiful, calm buildings and gardens full of carvings, statues and fountains for women and children who were survivors of violence. There was poetry and dancing. And — of course — the conference ended with a powerful candle-lit vigil for two hours at a busy crossroads in central Bangalore, with the theme of No More Wars, No More Violence.

Women in Black India continue to campaign and hold vigils in Bangalore, as they describe on their website:

> Black is the colour that we wear, Black, the colour that speaks our resistance. Silence is the language that we speak, Silence, a language that voices our anguish. In March 1993, inspired by the worldwide Women in Black movement, *Vimochana* initiated the first Women in Black action in Bangalore, India. Women in the city stood in silence protesting the razing of the *Babri Masjid* in *Ayodhya* and the communal conflict that spread in India. *Ayodhya* became a metaphor for the violent politics of Hindu Nationalism. Women stood protesting and remembering in silence the innocent victims, refusing to let the politics of hatred and intolerance destroy the humanity that binds and lives within all faiths. Women in Black India, in a quiet, sustained way, has sought to make public the many forms of 'personal' violence against women — wife battering, dowry deaths, female foeticide, female circumcision, pornography, sexual assault, rape. Everywhere, women are unmasking the many horrific faces of more public 'legitimate' violence — state repression, communalism, ethnic cleansing, nationalism, nuclearisation, wars … violence in the name of development, in the name of reproductive technologies, genetic engineering, and the

feminisation of poverty. The issues have been many. The forms in which protests have been expressed have also been varied. Silence, posters, placards, pamphlets and sometimes lighting lamps, have been an expression of this collective rebellion and resistance. While the above-mentioned issues are some of the vigils that the WIB India have focused on, we have also stood in solidarity for peoples living in war and conflict zones — with people of Afghanistan, Iraq, Palestine, to mention a few. Recent actions include:

- A candlelight vigil for Ankit Saxena — a victim of honour killing who was murdered by the family of his girlfriend, because they pursued their inter-faith relationship against the strong objections of her family, who disapproved of his religious identity. A candlelight vigil was held by Women in Black, *Vimochana*. The intention was to stand in silence and rebel against conformity that perpetuates patriarchy, casteism, fascism and religious fanaticism.

- A campaign for Ashifa: the rape of all human values. Nothing could evoke such widespread anguish and outrage as did the rape and murder of the eight-year-old cowherd Ashifa in Kathua, Jammu and Kashmir. Citizen groups, Resident Welfare Associations, Sports Federation, housewives and retired people turned out in large numbers at the Town Hall. As we gathered as Women in Black, as we made our protests public, we also mourned the loss of Ashifa.[6]

The Courts of Women travel to former Yugoslavia

At the same time as the Bangalore Court of Women, the idea had travelled to Sarajevo. A Women's Court was organised by Women in Black, Serbia, starting in 2015 with: Mothers of the Enclaves of Srebrenica; *Žepa* Women's Forum; Foundation CURE, Bosnia and Herzegovina; Centre for Women's Studies and Centre for Women War Victims — ROSA, Croatia; Kosovo Women's Network; National Council for Gender Equality, Macedonia; Anima, Montenegro; Women's Lobby, Slovenia; and Women's Studies (Amnesty International 2017). A lawyer who attended described it as follows:

What is critical about the Women's Court in Sarajevo was the way it was constructed for and with the full participation of women victims themselves. Women designed the court. Women testified. Women were the experts and judges ... the organizers provid[ed] support to victims before, during and after the court met ... [w]omen testified courageously of their experiences of losing family members to massacres, of mass rape and kidnapping, and of ethnic persecution. This feminist re-imagining of a court in which women victims are the central focus was very inspiring and thought-provoking to me as an international lawyer.[7]

Corinne Kumar gave a speech on the Feminist View of the Political Violence in India and South Africa and the Courts of Women at the seventeenth Women in Black Gathering, on the theme of 'Displaced Lives', in Cape Town, South Africa from 6-8 March 2018.

Women In Black South Africa: Displaced Lives

The seed of Women in Black South Africa (WiBSA) was planted during the first Women in Black demonstration in South Africa on 8 March 2001, in support of the *World Court of Women Against War, for Peace* organised by Corinne Kumar, which was being held in a Cape Town township at the same time. Hundreds of women from all over South Africa were joined by women from Bosnia, Palestine and India outside the Cape Town Civic Centre, dressed in black, with placards chanting 'No to violence!'.

However, the Women in Black group in South Africa was not officially started until April 2007, after a group of students and staff selected by the Gender Equity Unit at the University of the Western Cape had attended the World Social Forum in

Nairobi and were inspired by Women in Black there. Lameez Lalkhen, WiBSA, describes their aims in her summary of the WiB international conference in South Africa in 2018:

> Our objective is to raise awareness of the pervasiveness of systemic, state, social and domestic violence. We actively oppose injustice, poverty and all forms of violence. We resist all forms of aggression and work for a world where differences do not mean inequality or exclusion. We hold silent protest vigils and wear black to draw attention to the many forms of militarism, exploitation and oppression on our continent and elsewhere, to express solidarity with those who continue to suffer as a consequence of these.

WiBSA hosted the XVII WiB International Gathering in South Africa in 2018. The overarching theme of the International Gathering was Displaced Lives. Displacement is normally seen as forced geographical relocation due to various factors, mainly war, violence and persecution, and natural disasters. However, experiences of displacement are not bound by place, space or time. With more than 100 participants from Afghanistan, Armenia, Austria, Belgium, Colombia, Democratic Republic of Congo, Ethiopia, India, Israel, Rwanda, Somalia, Spain, South Africa, Sri Lanka, Switzerland, Tunisia, United Kingdom, United States of America, Uruguay, Western Sahara, and Zimbabwe, we shared the lived effects of forced displacement in all its forms and meanings, including emotional, psychological and spiritual displacement.

We live in a time when the Syrian civil uprising has been crushed and a brutal war of global proportions is waged against civilians, whether they remain or flee towards Europe and the uncertainties that holds. We also live in a time when South Africa's long history of displacement now also includes hosting those experiences of forced migration that our sisters and brothers on the continent experience. The City of Cape Town bears testimony to this history, from colonial conquest and slavery to the Apartheid forced removals, to the significant presence of a large number of people from other parts of Africa and South-East Asia, to the current struggle around displacement of poor people due to 'gentrification' in certain areas of the city. (Lameez Lalkhen, WiBSA, report from the WiB international conference in South Africa in 2018)

The XVII WiB International Gathering fostered dialogue about displacement in all its forms, between women across deep class, colour, faith and ideological divisions, in order to address the legacies of racism, hatred and class/power interests that underpin the current forms of systemic violence in South Africa and globally.

The aims of the conference were:

- to break the isolation between activists imposed by state borders, through exchange of strategies, tactics, concepts, methodologies and practices, with the aim of tackling the multiple challenges of forced displacement, as well as maintaining the WiB network by means of supporting women activists of different generations.
- to promote dialogue between feminist activists, both local and the international network of Women in Black, to reflect on the multiple forms of displacement between women belonging to diverse social classes, ethnicities, religious beliefs and ideological positions, with the aim of confronting the inheritance of racism, hatred and class/power interests which are at the base of current forms of systematic violence in South Africa and at global level. (Lameez Lalkhen, WiBSA, report from the WiB international conference in South Africa in 2018)

South African speakers at the conference talked about how colonial and Apartheid rule had been formally defeated, but post-apartheid macroeconomic policies sustained and deepened the systemic inequalities of capitalism. Women continue to bear the brunt of social and economic structures and policies that are anti-poor, racist and unjust. WiBSA is a pan-African, feminist, anti-war group. It also sees structural violence, together with racism, poverty and economic policies that promote inequality and displacement, as a form of war against ordinary people.

Women in Black South Africa denounced the violence of war, torture, rape, demolishment of homes, disappearances, rights abuses and misogyny. Their mandate is through silent protest to raise awareness and stand in solidarity with people in areas of violent conflict wherever they may be. WIBSA's main objectives are to bring an end to a culture of violence; actively oppose injustice, poverty and all forms of violence; and resist all forms of aggression.

Sessions at the conference discussed the shared activities of Women in Black in Colombia and Spain; similarities between apartheid South Africa and the state of Israel; Women, gentrification and displacement in Cape Town; Disarming patriarchy: Feminist Peace activism, #Metoo and non-violent resistance; Quadruple Jeopardy: displacement of black, working-class mothers of children with disabilities; Enemy Creation; Political Violence in India and South Africa — A Feminist View; Climate Change and LGBTI+ migrancy; Civil Activism in the Palestinian Struggle: from militarism to feminism; and Self-care as resistance.

Kwara Kekana talked about working with the Boycott, Divestment and Sanctions campaign in South Africa (BDS South Africa), a non-violent resistance movement called for by Palestinian civil society organisations since 2005, to engage the international community in the effort to bring justice to the Palestinian people. She raised the increased urgency for BDS and highlighted the similarities between apartheid South Africa and Israel, and also the occupation in the Western Sahara. The Israeli government continued to expand settlements on land confiscated from Palestinians and designated by international law as part of the state of Palestine. The economic, academic and cultural campaign aimed to bring an end to these 'apartheid' policies and violations of international law. Participants in the session agreed that WiB must take a stand together for Boycott, Divestment and Sanctions.

WiB from Colombia and Spain emphasised that violence against women and challenges and hardships for refugees are still prevalent in both countries. In Colombia, narco-trafficking, violence against women, torture and kidnap are ongoing. WiB worked for truth, justice and reparation; to keep the memory of all those who have been displaced alive; and to help and support the peace process.

Some of the other sessions included poetry, painting, dancing, singing, and a historical walking tour of the sites of slavery, class, and dispossession in Cape Town. The conference ended with a march to the Houses of Parliament for social justice and against the violence of displacement, and a peaceful protest that demonstrated a collective of the women of the world supporting one another in creating a better future for the next generation.

Once again, the international conference in South Africa broke new ground for WiB, deepening and widening understanding of the ways that militarism, colonialism and racism intersect with displacement and damage to the environment. Participants in the Colombia/Spanish workshop talked about the importance of women working across borders together, and proposed that:

- all the work done by WiB and the Courts of Women should be documented.

- violence against women has increased; we need to move on to working on peace beyond the masculinist definition and understanding of war — peace is not about the absence of war, but about home, health, food, dignity. This should be written about!

(Lameez Lalkhen, WiBSA, report from the WiB international conference in South Africa in 2018)

NOTES

1   Much of the description of *Vimochana* and related institutions
     in Bangalore in this chapter derive from a research visit Cynthia
     Cockburn made there in 2004/5 (Cockburn 2007). Some direct
     quotations come from unpublished Research Profiles, some of which
     are available on Cynthia's website, www.cynthiacockburn.org This
     quotation comes from 'Violence as indivisible: Women in Black,
     Vimochana and the Asian Women's Human Rights Council, Bangalore,
     India', Research Profile No.11, 7 April, 2005.

2   A partial list of some other Courts of Women includes:
     The 1995 *Arab Women's Court* in Beirut, Lebanon, on violence against
     women. In 1996 the *Mahkamate El Nissa El Arabiya* (Permanent Arab
     Women's Court) was established.
     The *Court of Women International War Crimes Tribunal on Japan's
     Military Sexual* Slavery was held in 2000, convened to gather testimony
     from victims, and then to try groups and individuals for rape or sexual
     slavery i.e., forcing women to sexually service Japanese soldiers.
     The World Court of Women Against War, for Peace was held March
     8, 2001 in Cape Town, South Africa to bear witness to the enormous
     violence and genocide caused by wars around the world. 4,000 people
     from around South Africa and the world participated.
     A *World Court of Women on U.S. War Crimes* took place in Mumbai,
     India, on January 18, 2004, as part of the 2004 World Social Forum.
     The 36th Court of Women, *Daughters of Fire : The Indian Court of
     Women on Dowry and Related Forms of Violence Against Women* was
     held in Bangalore, India on July 26–29, 2009.
     The *Southeast Asia Court of Women on HIV and Human Trafficking* was
     held on August 6, 2009 during the 9th International Congress on AIDS
     in Asia and the Pacific (ICAAP) in Bali.
     *World Court of Women on Poverty in the United States: Disappeared in
     America* was the first US example, held in California, USA, from May
     10–13, 2012. Representing the western region of the country, the focus
     was on poverty in the U.S. In 2013, another World Court of Women
     was held in Philadelphia, Pennsylvania, again focused on poverty.

3   Summary Report from the World Court of Women Against War, For
     Peace, XVI Biennial Women in Black Conference, 15 – 19 November
     2015, Bangalore, India

4   Cathy Otten, *Guardian*, 25.7.17

5   Dr Rosalie Bertell, 1985 *No Immediate Danger: Prognosis for a
     Radioactive Earth*, The Women's Press, London

6   https://www.vimochana.co.in/ (accessed 10.6.21)

7   Interview with Karima Bennoune, reproduced from Peace is Loud,
     20 May 2015, http://www.zenskisud.org/en/pdf/Karima_Bennoune_
     (Interview)_eng.pdf (accessed 19 July 2021) quoted in Amnesty
     International Report, 2017.

CHAPTER 6

WOMEN IN BLACK IN CENTRAL AND SOUTH AMERICA

Like South Africa, the South American nation of Colombia has known more decades of deadly civil strife than almost any other country in the world. The London-based NGO Conciliation Resources wrote that the Colombian conflict has been not only of long duration but 'overwhelming in its complexity and devastating in its impact'. They note that the country's homicide rate was among the highest anywhere (González 2004:10-17). It's perhaps not surprising, then, that Colombia is home to one of the world's most sustained and impassioned women's movements against violence and war. The organisation which gave rise to Women in Black in Colombia is *La Ruta Pacífica de las Mujeres por la Negociación de los Conflictos* (Women's Peaceful Road for the Negotiation of Conflicts): *La Ruta Pacífica* or RPM for short. It is with their story that this chapter on WiB's spread from Israel Palestine to South and Central America begins.

La Ruta Pacífica came into existence in 1996, a nationwide, pacifist and feminist movement, with a presence in 142 municipalities across nine regions of Colombia (Bolívar, Santander, Bogotá, Valle del Cauca, Putumayo, Cauca, Risaraldo, Chocó and Antioquia). It has a complicated structure, comprising 300 organisations, and involving as many as 10,000 women. Much of their effort and activity has gone into exposing the impact of armed conflict on women's lives and gaining understanding and recognition of the efforts women make, despite the violence, to maintain the social fabric of their communities. A second aim, more difficult and demanding, has been to incorporate women, their experiences of conflict and their interest in peace, into successive rounds of negotiation between the government and the various insurgent groups.

Before looking more closely at how *La Ruta Pacífica* works and how they have enabled and activated Women in Black in Colombia, let's sketch the history of the country's wars. Colombia sits on the northern coastline of South America, adjacent to Panama, bordered by Venezuela to the north-east (on the Atlantic coast) and Ecuador to the south-west (on the Pacific shore). Spanish explorers arrived in South America at the end of the fifteenth century CE and 'settlement' followed during the sixteenth century. As elsewhere, colonisation of the region that would become Colombia was imposed on the indigenous peoples by force of arms. Once established, the colonists turned and fought the Spanish empire for independence. This was achieved in 1819, but it was not the end of violence. From the middle of the nineteenth century, two major parties, the Liberals and the Conservatives, competed for control of Colombia. A bitter ten-year war between them, termed *La Violencia*, took place in the mid-twentieth century (Gonzalez, 2004).

La Ruta Pacífica was not born, however, until the end of the twentieth century. And by then, the nature of the violence scarring the country had changed yet again. Now the Colombian government itself was being challenged by various guerrilla forces representing class interests. In 1964 a leftist National Liberation Army (the ELN), a Maoist People's Liberation Army (the EPL) and an even more significant guerrilla force, the Revolutionary Armed Forces of Colombia (FARC), associated with the Communist Party, were founded. In 1971 another leftist force formed — the 'M-19' guerrillas. These guerrilla forces were spurred into activity by poverty, inequality, the unconstrained power of the big landowners and the elitism of the political class. The guerrillas initially gained support for egalitarian social and economic programmes, particularly in areas of the country where the exploitation of workers and peasants was giving rise to the greatest resentment. Their cause was justified, but they funded their activities by exploitation, kidnapping and levies on the production and sale of cocaine, grown in large quantities in Colombia. The government's armed forces killed, imprisoned and tortured tens of thousands in the course of fighting the guerrillas. Sometimes they killed innocent citizens and placed weapons on their corpses, in order to claim they were guerrillas (Human Rights Watch World Report on Colombia, 2021).

The state's inability to destroy the guerrillas led wealthy landowners and the capitalist class to raise and fund their own armed forces, paramilitary militias that came together in the early 1980s in the United Self-Defence Forces *(Autodefensas Unidas de Colombia - AUC)*. The USA compounded the violence by contributing massively to the Colombian government's resources and forces with the aim of securing the region against left-wing insurgency, protecting oil reserves and other business interests, and stemming the flow of narcotics to the USA.

Poverty, lack of prospects and fear for their families had driven people to enlist in one force or another. More than 11,000 children were estimated to have been forcibly enrolled into either guerrilla or paramilitary forces. And many women were among the fighters too. According to the paramilitary AUC, women comprised 12 per cent of their ranks; the estimate for FARC was as high as 40 per cent. During the 1990s the annual number of violent deaths ranged between 25,000 and 30,000, representing a national figure of 80 per 100,000 inhabitants, one of the highest rates recorded anywhere. At least 13 per cent had been political murders perpetrated by state agents or members of armed groups, mainly against civilians (Meertens 2001).

Sexual violence against women was widespread, used by state forces, paramilitaries and guerrillas as a weapon of war to punish women for associating with 'the wrong side' or indirectly to punish and humiliate the enemy. Women, too, predominated among the huge numbers of displaced people. Violence associated with the conflicts has forcibly displaced more than eight million Colombians since 1985 (Human Rights Watch, 2021).

Moves towards peace

In the early 1990s, movements for peace emerged, first in the most war-ravaged areas such as Urabá (in Antioquia) and Magdalena Medio. A Committee for the Search for Peace was formed, and the Catholic Church set up a National Conciliation Commission. A significant initiative was the creation of *Redepaz*, a National Network of Initiatives for Peace and Against War, which in 1997 organised a referendum that brought in ten million votes for peace and eventually led to mass demonstrations around the country involving an estimated eight million people united under the slogan *No Más* (No More) (Rodriguez 2004). Many of the peace activists were women. Olga Amparo Sánchez Gómez, a feminist academic and anti-war activist, describes this mobilisation as the third of three great 'leaps forward' for Colombian women. It was, she said, as significant as winning the vote over fifty years earlier and achieving a reform of gender aspects of the Constitution in 1991. With working-class and peasant movements crushed by the state, women's organisations were important bearers of democratic demands. Patricia Prieto, of the *Grupo Mujer y Sociedad* (Women and Society Group) said: 'It's on women's shoulders. They are holding things together. They are the weavers and maintainers of the social fabric' (Cockburn 2007:18).

In 1998, Andrés Pastrana was elected president of Colombia, and began peace talks with the guerrillas. First, in 1999, negotiations began with FARC, and continued in stop-start fashion for some years. They were broken off in 2002. Under the next president, Alvaro Uribe, talks began between the government and the AUC paramilitaries, and then in 2005 with the second biggest left-wing guerrilla group, the ELN. In 2012, a new round of peace talks between the Colombian state, now led by

Manuel Santos, and FARC began, and a deal ending 52 years of armed conflict was eventually signed in 2016. The peace accord brought an initial decline in violence, but conflict-related violence has since taken new forms. Across the region, former paramilitary groups, drug-trafficking organisations and former FARC militia members are using massacres to resolve disputes. Community leaders and human rights defenders played a key role in representing the interests of ordinary people during the implementation of the peace deal and remain vital to the fabric of social life after the war. But these are the people being murdered in large numbers, especially in rural areas. If the Colombian government had continued in denial, the 2016 peace agreement was under severe threat (Hood, 2021). A new President, Gustavo Petro, has now been elected (August 2022) and promises to make Colombia's peace deal a priority.

La Ruta Pacífica has contributed substantially to the peace movement. They are more outspokenly pacifist than most other women's NGOs in Colombia, and uncompromising in their rejection of the use of armed force on any pretext. They excuse neither the state and its paramilitaries, nor the guerrilla organisations. They make no exceptions in the name of 'just wars'. They are holistic in their analysis, calling for economic redistribution and protection of the environment, and quite explicitly feminist, using the concepts of patriarchy and patriarchalism unhesitatingly. Within the embrace of *La Ruta* are several substantial associations, including *Vamos Mujer* (Woman Let's Go) and *Mujeres que Crean* (Creative Women), both based in Medellín. Membership of *La Ruta* is also open to individuals, and their intention is to ensure the inclusion and representation of women of all the main cultures of Colombia, including those of the many indigenous tribes, Afro-Colombian women who are the descendants of slaves, peasant women, young women, academics and women of the urban poor.

Cynthia Cockburn visited the main office of RPM in Bogotá and interviewed women there about their politics. First and foremost, they saw themselves as fostering peaceful resistance to militarist violence, 'that redeems the sacred value of life and thence of the "everyday", of sensibility, the respect for difference, solidarity and sisterhood'. They sought linkages at various levels in the form of local, urban and regional dialogue within the populations most affected by the armed conflict. They also sought women's active participation in the national process of negotiation leading to a peaceful route out of conflict. They were calling for a culture of non-violence and co-existence, and using international human rights, especially women's rights, as a rallying point. They were demanding processes of memory, truth, justice and reparation because 'only these could permit the recovery of hope and the process of reconciliation in our country' (Cockburn 2007:19).

Dating from their very first action in 1996, *La Ruta* has used a slogan that recalls the women's strategy against war in Aristophanes' play *Lysistrata* (from the first millennium BCE). '*No parimos hijos ni hijas para la guerra*': 'we won't give birth to sons or daughters for war.' It was Rocío Pineda who had the idea for that. She invited women to question themselves: Who are these men we love? Whose are these bodies that we desire? How can we take into our arms someone who has killed, who has left some child fatherless? Women, Rocío felt, should use the significant power they have to turn men from militarism and war (Cockburn 2007:19).

The work of *La Ruta Pacífica de las Mujeres*

La Ruta Pacífica was characterised from the start by a strategy of mass mobilisations, bringing women from every corner of the country to offer solidarity to those in war-afflicted regions. The first mobilisation was in 1996, the year of its formation, which transported 2,000 women in forty coaches from all over Colombia to the strife-ridden area of Urabá (Antioquia Department). They chose 25 November, the international day of action against violence against women, for this convergence

— one that took some of them several days of travel. Another mobilisation, even more ambitious, took 3,500 women in 98 coaches to Putumayo, a coca-growing area in the south, deeply affected by the anti-narcotics programme. In these and other actions, the women gave a lot of thought to symbolism. The trope of 'weaving' recurred, representing connectedness. Unravelling the web and weaving anew symbolised the creative cycle of life, death and renewal. They flagged up colour — yellow for truth, white for justice, green for hope, blue for making amends, purple for memory and orange for peaceful resistance. They were inventing a new visual and textual language, and — to great effect – making videos, using the media creatively.

La Ruta were working intensively on two fronts. First, at a basic level, they were consistently active in protection and care, giving psychosocial support and spiritual nurture to women survivors and victims of the different kinds of violence they were experiencing in Colombia. Secondly, they were training and developing women to be politically effective. The clearest example of this was the huge effort they put into their 'Women's Truth Commission', *La Comisión de la Verdad desde las Mujeres para Colombia*, initiated in 2010. They trained twenty-seven interviewers in a method of action research, in which by effective listening they could offer women a space in which to unburden themselves, to make visible and record their experiences and their suffering. More than 1,000 individual testimonies were recorded, besides those of members of nine women's organisations, one in each of the regions where RPM had an office. This major piece of work took several years to complete. Its methodology was meticulously described in a book entitled *Memoria para la Vida* (Ruta Pacífica 2013).

Importantly, the Women's Truth Commission was a prompt for the eventual National Commission for the Elucidation of Truth that began work in 2018. The latter contains three or four individuals who had been associated with *La Ruta*. Teresa Aristizábal (one of the coordinators of *Ruta Pacífica* in

Antioquia) said that they had been able, through these members, to feed some of the Women's Truth Commission findings into the processes of the official Commission, and to share with them their research methodology. It is interesting to note that the *Ruta* Women's Truth Commission combines both the kinds of activism characteristic of *La Ruta* — it was simultaneously training and developing women for political effectiveness and providing an example of the protection and care of women: the act of unburdening themselves to the Commission's interviewers, as Teresa pointed out, was a process of healing for these many women witnesses.[1]

Clara Mazo López (a *Ruta Pacífica* activist in Antioquia), said that Colombian women managed to get women and women's interests inserted into the peace process between the government and the FARC guerrillas.[2] In 2013, *La Ruta* and several other women's networks organised the 'First National Summit of Women and Peace', and as a result a Gender Subcommission was added into the dialogue and negotiations that were being held in Havana the following year. This resulted in an unforeseen element in the peace agreement of July 2016, a 'Gender Accord'. Clara remembers that Colombian media reported that this was the only time such a thing had occurred in the world. In 2016 women's organisations called a second Summit in which they analysed the gender aspects of the accord and explored the ways in which women's groups could help to implement the agreement's programmes at local level. Clara noted that between 2017 and 2018 they had participated alongside various social organisations in a new process of government negotiations with the other significant guerrilla organisation, the ELN, resulting in a three-month ceasefire.

During this process RPM had meetings with the 'peace managers' of the ELN incarcerated in Bellavista prison in Medellín. The aim was to develop a full understanding of the situation of ELN female members held in prison and try to ensure these women could participate in the peace dialogues in Quito, Ecuador. Unfortunately, when President Ivan Duque took office in 2018, the negotiations began to break down and in February 2019 the ELN launched a cruel attack on a Police Cadet Academy, causing several deaths by burning, and rupturing the fragile agreement. *La Ruta* spoke out emphatically against this.

La Ruta's embrace of Women in Black

La Ruta Pacífica started carrying out monthly WiB vigils in 2000, in most of its regions, just after the *Ruta* and the *Organización Femenina de Barrancabermeja* (Women's Organisation of Barrancabermeja) jointly created the National Movement of Women Against War. Their chosen day and time for vigils is the last Tuesday of every month, in the late afternoon. They adopted the black-clad, silent and motionless form practised by WiB internationally. Teresa Aristizábal, coordinator of *La Ruta* and WiB in Antioquia, described their 'doing' of Women in Black:

> We heard about WiB in 2000. That's when we started doing the vigils, and we have done them 'religiously' for nineteen years. Even if it rains, even when we have had a crisis, we've done the vigils. It's totally part of us.
>
> We call the vigils *plantón de Mujeres de Negro,* because we plant ourselves in a public place, where many will see us. During the vigils the two names coexist — *Ruta Pacífica* and WiB — because we are twin sisters. The vigil is a political and symbolic act. It's an international pact between women, it's an expression of our feminist identity. We get inspiration for our political actions from WiB, from their silence and wearing black. This is the action that brings us together with the political principles of WiB around the world.
>
> When we do the vigils, we get re-energised. When we have almost no hope and we hold a vigil, we renew our

hope. The vigil is a moment of hope, joy and sorrow also. It's a way to tell people that *Ruta Pacífica* and WiB exist and that we are advocating for a peaceful country, that women's lives and bodies have been the most affected.

When vigils have been suspended because of security issues, we anyhow know that being together in the street, making noise and saying that we belong to an international movement, give us protection. Women standing together and wearing black locally, nationally and internationally, is our protection. WiB give us protection. We say with a lot of pride that we are part of the international movement called Women in Black and this generates respect among politicians, journalists, etc.

The international meeting in Bogotá in 2011 was such a thing! A historical event! The *encuentro* (conference) was the chance to see the sisterhood and solidarity that other women feel for Colombia, to feel that our work was understood and appreciated by women around the world. A long-term effect of the *encuentro* is that when we are feeling down, when we ask ourselves which direction Colombia is taking, we tell each other: let's not forget the women of Sarajevo, let's not forget the women of Palestine, let's not forget the women who have also lived through war, and that immediately makes us alive. We just need to say: Women in Black, and we stand up from wherever we are! (Teresa Aristizábal interview with Adriana Medina Lalinde, 2019)

Teresa's group mounted vigils in Berrío Park, in the city of Medellín, the capital of Antioquia, and sometimes, additionally, in smaller towns in the region. All the other eight regional organisations of *La Ruta Pacífica* were similarly the sites of monthly vigils. They called their vigils by the Spanish word *plantones*. A '*planton*' signifies a long wait, a standing, as on duty. But they do not only stand. Teresa went on to say, 'We do pedagogical theatre, we do art with our bodies. We read a short statement and then we "sing" our well-known slogans. Usually we are around 40 women. We wear black, even when it's sunny and super-hot!' She explained, 'Wearing black is very important to us. Black means sorrow, mourning. We are saying "I am the voice of women who are no longer here. I feel the pain of other women." We are standing in solidarity and sisterhood with other women.' On the other hand, they use a particular symbolic object — a fishnet decorated with coloured flags and butterflies. They light large candles, and bring water in a vessel, and soil from the various territories. As well as the universal theme of resistance to militarism combined with resistance against violence against women (*No a la guerra y a las violencias contra las mujeres*), the tropes of the vigils fit particular regions. For instance, in impoverished Chocó, where 85 per cent of the population is Afro-Colombian and indigenous, they protest against racism, displacement and disadvantage (the central government provides almost no public funds for this region). In parched Medellín, they feature the water shortage, water rights and the privatisation of water supplies.

> The vigils are very appreciated by activists here in Antioquia. Recently, I was planning a visit to Anorí, such an isolated and small town north-east of Antioquia, you have to drive seven hours through bumpy roads to get there. And the women's group there said that we must organize a WiB vigil there. They insisted that it 'just wasn't possible' that women of *La Ruta* and Women in Black were visiting the town and would not hold a vigil. Imagine that! (Teresa Aristizábal interview with Adriana Medina Lalinde, 2019)

Clara Mazo López adds more about *La Ruta Pacífica* and its Women in Black activities:

> *La Ruta Pacífica* has had particularly close links with the Women in Black groups in Italy and Spain. At the start

of 2017, soon after the signing of the accords with FARC, a group of RPM travelled to Italy, invited to speak about women in the context of the Colombian peace process. A particularly strong relationship developed with Patricia Tough, a member of *Donne in Nero*, Italy. The latter accompanied an RPM group on a visit to Chile to talk about the Colombian experience and motivate Chilean women to create WiB there. Teresa was one of those who travelled and helped them understand that what we are doing is also done in many other places around the world to oppose war. (Clara Mazo Lopez interview with Adriana Medina Lalinde, 2019)

WiB International Encuentro XV

When *La Ruta Pacífica* decided to offer to facilitate the next international WiB biennial conference (*encuentro*) in Bogotá, the invitation was welcomed with alacrity by WiB in over thirty different countries.[3] It was especially pleasing to anticipate meeting for the first time in South America. The various delegations were invited to bring statements about their situations, to bring letters from those left behind, and above all to bring photos — of their circumstances, their members, their actions. *La Ruta* reminded everyone of the demands and objectives of the International WiB Network, which would be restated and embodied in this next *encuentro*:

> To speak for ourselves, refuse to be enemies, bear witness to women's suffering, build bridges between women, make women's voices heard in places of power, make them take women's demands into account, obtain participation in negotiations for resolution of armed conflict, be involved in lawsuits against war criminals, spread information, actively participate in every forum for peace, and create measures for the eradication of violence, and engage in peace education.[4]

This XVth *encuentro* took place on 15-20 August 2011, in Bogotá, the Colombian capital. Around 240 women attended, including 160 from Colombia and 80 from fifteen other countries: Bosnia-Herzegovina, Congo, Ecuador, Honduras, India, Israel, Italy, Mexico, Palestine, Peru, Serbia, Spain, the UK, Uruguay and the USA. The biggest groups came from Italy and Spain, countries that had already, as we have seen, developed productive connections with the Colombian women of *La Ruta Pacífica*.[5]

Sue Finch, the UK delegate, reported that:

The official welcome for international women was held on the afternoon of Monday 15 August with four mime artists (*Las Mima-Hadas*) giving each woman flowers, tying black threads round our wrists (we were invited to make a wish that would come true when the bracelet fell off), and leading us to registration bags full of gifts (soap, map of Bogotá, programme, badges etc. — all with the beautiful *encuentro* logo). So the welcome was wonderfully warm, and transcended language barriers. Midday Tuesday, the first day of work, began with a welcome for Colombian participants. Each was given an olive branch and presents. One woman from each of the nine regions of Colombia presented something symbolic, and then one woman from each of the sixteen countries represented stood in a circle and blew out a candle, while Clara, from Medellín, sounded peace bells. Next we watched a film on WiB *encuentros* of the past, contributed by Spanish women, and listened to a 'song of friendship' by Colombian women. Then Marina Gallego Zapata, the National Coordinator of *La Ruta Pacífica*, opened the *encuentro* with an introduction outlining the key themes. The first three she emphasised were rebellion, empathy and solidarity. Then came: addressing the structural causes of war; strengthening WiB at local, national and international levels; and WiB support for the pursuit of negotiated solutions to armed conflict in Colombia.

In the opening panel that afternoon, one of the panellists, Palestinian Darin Khattab, talked about intersectionality as a tool to help analyse women's complex and different experiences. The concept, she explained, was first used in the US in 1989 to describe women's employment. In her context she felt it could help us understand how thirty-six years of Israeli occupation of the West Bank and Gaza had fragmented Palestinian women's experiences, with huge implications for identity. For example, there were differences between the multiple and compound layers of disadvantage and oppression experienced by: a Palestinian woman who lives in a Lebanese refugee camp and dreams of going back to Palestinian lands; a Palestinian woman who lives in Jordan and has similar dreams of 'return'; a woman who lives in Gaza, oppressed by the Hamas government as well as by Israel; her imagined sister, who lives in the West Bank; and finally, Darin herself, a Palestinian woman who lives in the Israeli part of Jerusalem and has citizenship of the Israeli state. All these women have totally different realities — yet all live in a patriarchal and militarised society. Each woman might also be a victim of domestic violence. Darin described how, growing up, her front yard had been simultaneously the back yard of an Israeli neighbourhood. She had not been allowed to play outside. The Occupation had led to poor communication. If people lived on different sides of checkpoints, there was no way to visit each other. The Palestinian Authority, for its part, she said, paid very little attention to women's issues.

The second panellist on Tuesday afternoon was Piedad Córdoba, a lawyer and until recently a Senator in the Colombian National Congress. Notably, and illegally, she had been thrown out of the Congress for her views on peace. Piedad stressed war as a women's issue. 'Women have always been the spoils of war,' she said. 'The armed conflict of the last fifty years in Colombia has had worsening consequences for women, increasingly involving sexual violence.' She described how women are raped in police stations if they come to report an attack — or they are told, 'that's not our problem, it's a private matter'. Women may be raped and murdered if they offend their husband — or their husband's enemy. Hospitals, doctors and nurses cannot report injuries because in doing so they risk death themselves. Child prostitution has increased rapidly, with 'virgin vaginas' offered for sale to foreigners through networks operating out of ports. War had de-railed and re-routed resources that should be going to education and other services that are vital for women and their children — and this in a country in which 20 million out of a population of 46 million live in poverty. But women throughout history have played an important role in resolving conflicts, Piedad stressed.

On the third day of the Bogotá *encuentro*, 'testimonies' were delivered from a number of different countries. Among them, Celine Sugana spoke from India. She told how Women in Black had started in Bangalore in 1993, and that their Thursday vigils opposed communal violence, conflicts over water and land, police brutality and 'dowry killings' in families. Growing violence in the home, she said, was linked to the hyper-masculinisation of Indian society. There was ever more rape, sexual harassment, female infanticide and foeticide. There were as many as five 'unnatural deaths in marriage' in Bangalore every week. India was a poor and caste-ridden country, in which Dalits (or Untouchables) were oppressed. And in spite of this poverty, India was a nuclear-armed state.

Corinne Kumar (founder and Coordinator of the World Courts of Women and Secretary General of El Taller, an international NGO committed to working with civil society organisations to address issues of poverty, underdevelopment and women's rights, also a founding member of the Centre for Informal Development Studies, of the Asian Women's Human Rights Council and of *Vimochana*, an NGO in Bangalore concerned with domestic violence, dowry-related deaths and workplace sexual harassment) was also present in Bogota among the Indian women, and showed a film about the 'Courts of Women'.

Beatrice from the Panzi Hospital in the Democratic Republic of Congo (DRC) said that Colombia and Congo might be considered as 'twins'. Both had wonderful people, were richly diverse and had plentiful natural resources (oil, gold, copper). But in both contexts, the latter were exploited by multinational firms in such a way that 'everything that nature has given us now belongs to the great powers, and we live in almost slave-like conditions'. Rape had been extensively used in the Congo as a weapon of war, particularly since the effects of the 1994-6 war in neighbouring Rwanda spilled over into their country. Beatrice shocked the *encuentro* in describing the particular forms that have been taken by sexual violence — women raped in front of their husbands and children, fathers forced to rape their sons and daughters. 'They use sticks, weapons and fire in women's vaginas. Women who resist are raped. There have been fifty rapes at a time, continuing day and night, in the public square, with women cut and paraded like trophies, then killed and left in ditches.' But Congolese women resisted: they would not kneel; they stood up to denounce the violence and would continue to do so. You will see, Beatrice concluded, 'that though they are geographically far apart, Congo and Colombia are close in experience. From now on you have sisters in the DRC.'

Other speakers at the *encuentro* included Mirella Forel, from *Mujeres de Negro* in Spain; Marija Perkovic from Bosnia-Herzegovina; Jadranka Milocevic from Serbia; and Lulu Luz from the Philippines. There were also five Israeli Women in Black, including Yvonne Deutsch, Tamara Traubmann and Orla Nathan. These women all spoke movingly of their experiences in women's anti-violence and anti-war activism. Ria Convents came from Belgium to this — her twelfth — WiB *encuentro* and made sure that there was a positive input concerning the interests and activities of lesbian women in WiB. She recalled how at the first WiB conference in Israel in 1994, Hanna Safran had coordinated a lesbian workshop. 'The women's movement helped me to overcome internalised homophobia — part of militaristic and patriarchal society,' she said. Lulu Luz from the Philippines told how she had been working in Seattle, USA, as an advocate in sexual violence cases, and with sexually trafficked and incarcerated young people. 'Violence against lesbians,' she said, 'always increases in time of war.' Judith Berlowitz, from San Francisco, told how Women in Black in the USA had been inspired not only by Israeli WiB but also by the South African Black Sash movement[6] and the *Madres de la Plaza de Mayo* in Argentina. She said the aims of the Women in Black vigils in her city were to educate and inform the public, and to send letters to politicians — senators and congress-people. She would return from the *encuentro*, she said, with the intention of making a new start with their list-serve, organising a travelling WiB film festival and 'reassessing our activities with the aim of attracting younger women'.

Piedad Cordoba stressed in her closing address to the conference: 'Feminist politics does not only struggle to eradicate injustice, but to build alliances; to be subjects, not objects. Deconstructing patriarchal policies of war makes us conscientious objectors. We contribute to eradicating sexism and violence, and to opening dialogue. We have to take to the streets, to face terror, because we want a future without violence. We will work towards negotiated solutions to guarantee life, social justice, equality and respect. Even in the darkest times we have the right to expect light.' She said that the presence of so many participants from other countries, 'makes us feel that peace is more and more possible every day'.

On the final day, around three hundred women turned out for a vigil and a demonstration in central Bogotá. There were banners and placards in many languages. There was the decorated fishnet the group regularly deployed in their vigils, whistles, face-painting, and the laying out of huge hand-worked quilts representing women who had died in conflict, with symbolic crosses and caskets. A woman dressed in butterfly-garb danced to symbolise hope. Women from each region of Colombia spoke and crowds gathered to hear them and watch the drama.

Colombian women at the *encuentro* talked about how they had been inspired by being part of WiB, at the same time as they inspired WiB from across the world by demonstrating new ways of developing creativity, drama and symbolism in mass actions.

Women in Black in Uruguay

Women in Black got going in another South American country, Uruguay, about the same time as it did in Colombia. The two countries are far distant, Uruguay being tucked away on

the Atlantic shore between much larger neighbours, Brazil to
its north, and Argentina to its south and west. The website of
Mujeres de Negro de Uruguay notes that the women conduct
their vigils in black (which they describe as a sign of mourning,
and in order to make themselves noticeable); and in silence
(because there are no words that can express all that women
suffer in this world, and to denounce the historic absence of
women's voices).[7] Their vigils are repetitive, and formalised,
in a way that is by now familiar from many other countries.
But Uruguayan women add to their street-side visual effect a
white 'knot' or 'bow' to symbolise peace, and they consistently
display their recurrent theme: 'Every Death Matters' (*Ni Una
Muerte Indiferente*). The Uruguayan WiB website tells the world
that a fundamental purpose of their actions is the definitive and
absolute rejection of militarised societies and of armed conflict,
both of which they understand as supporting and reproducing
patriarchy. With their feminist and pacifist ethic they seek to
deconstruct a society based on relations of violence and replace
it with peaceful and respectful coexistence between people
with differences. They focus on violence experienced by women
in times of both peace and war.

Uruguay is the second smallest of South America's nations,
with an estimated population of three and a half million, of
whom almost two million live in the capital city, Montevideo.
Like Colombia and other Spanish colonies, from the seventeenth to the twentieth centuries the country experienced
endless violence, by Spanish colonisers against indigenous
people, the Charrúa, and later, between groups of European
colonisers and the European empires. However, the period of
violence that lives most acutely in the memory of WiB dates
from a military coup in 1973 which established a government
that persecuted socialists and other progressives and did not
give way to a democratic civilian government until 1985.
During these violent years a leftist guerrilla movement which
had existed since 1960 — the Tupamaros — provided the main

opposition, operating mostly in urban areas, particularly in Montevideo, assassinating police officers and other agents of the dictatorship. Today Uruguay is a comparatively peaceful country, with no terrorism, relative prosperity, socio-economic equality and press freedom. WiB (*Mujeres de Negro*) therefore directs opposition mainly to the kinds of violence experienced by women in everyday life. For this they blame 'patriarchalism', which they see expressed in the appropriation by men of women's bodies, their sexuality, their children, their wealth and their ideas through the creation of norms and laws, and interpersonal violence. Uruguayan women see women worldwide being tortured by genital mutilation and surgical interventions — especially, in the case of young women, in pursuit of 'beauty'. They blame the persistence and survival of patriarchy on the various dimensions of 'alienation' generated by their system of government and the power of Uruguay's wealth-owning class.

As in Colombia, where we saw that Women in Black flowers in *La Ruta Pacífica,* which associates under a single name a vast network of national and regional women's organisations, so in Uruguay *Mujeres de Negro* (MdN) list some seventeen organisations as being their partners and colleagues in action against gender violence, including *Mujer y Salud Uruguay* (MYSU — Women and Health), the *Comité de América Latina y el Caribe para la Defensa de los Derechos de la Mujer* (CLADEM — the Latin American and Caribbean Committee for the Defence of the Rights of Women), and *Red Contra la Violencia Doméstica y Sexual* (Network against Domestic and Sexual Violence, which includes 39 organisations).[8]

Jenny Escobar Iglesias from Women in Black in Uruguay had attended the *encuentro* in Bogotá in 2011. It was agreed there that the next *encuentro* would be organised by Uruguayan WiB in Montevideo. This came about as planned and took place from Monday 19 to Saturday 24 August 2013. Ana Valdés, a WiB who had survived torture under the military coup, helped to organise the event and translate. The *encuentro* was attended by sixty women from sixteen countries. Two women, Sue Finch and Liz Khan, travelled to Montevideo from London, and in their English-language report they provide the following account of the XVI *encuentro*.[9]

> The key themes for the 2013 *encuentro* were violence in the home, at work, on the streets, in war, and by UN 'peace-keeping' missions. Some women (particularly from Serbia) questioned whether violence in the home should be considered equally important as violence in armed conflict, but after difficult discussions it was agreed that both had to be addressed as part of a continuum of patriarchal violence.
>
> Jenny Escobar Iglesias welcomed the assembled women from the platform on the first morning. She said that 'if Montevideo was now a capital of peace it was so in part because of the work of *Mujeres de Negro*. In their country, one in three women are known to suffer from male violence, and they term the resulting high level of deaths 'femicide'. Jenny told how *Mujeres de Negro* had opened an office and received some funding from the government to organise the *encuentro*, had made alliances with other groups, including the White Ribbon Campaign (a men's anti-violence group), and had campaigned for a new law against violence against women. MdN presented the draft law and then a socialist congresswoman submitted it to the Executive and the law came into force in 2012. Jenny reckoned MdN (WiB) was currently working with around 150 women in Uruguay. Three and a half thousand women had come out on their most recent national demonstration, after three years of work.
>
> Ana Olivera was the second Uruguayan speaker. Then Mayor of Montevideo, she was the first woman to have been elected mayor in Uruguay (and since 2021 has

represented Montevideo in the Uruguay Assembly): 'We can proudly say that we are pioneers in relation to woman and peace. We have just achieved the designation of Montevideo as a "Peace City" by the Hiroshima-based Council of Cities for Peace. We have instigated the creation of a special free phone number, 0800, on which to report domestic violence. And we have created Women's Councils in many areas of Montevideo to support women within their localities.'

Ana had arranged for the conference attendees to visit one of the nine *Comunas de Mujer* in the city, where they learned of the legal and counselling support these offered. Lilian Abracinskas, another local woman, told us that abortion was even now only permitted in Uruguay up to the twelfth week of pregnancy, and thus was in reality for most purposes still a crime. But there had been advances in gay rights, and in general some cultural liberalisation. However, Alicia Esquivel, a doctor working at the Ministry of Social Development, reported that people of African descent were earning 27 per cent less than other Uruguayans, and tended to be in unqualified work due to widespread discrimination. 'Let's eradicate racism!' she said. (unpublished report by Sue Finch and Liz Khan of London Women in Black on their return from the XVI *encuentro* in Montevideo in 2013.)

As at the *encuentro* in Bogotá two years previously, there were presentations at the Montevideo conference by women from many countries — including Argentina, Armenia, Belgium, Chile, the Congo, Guatemala, India, Serbia, UK and USA. Two women spoke from the USA: one of them — Margaret Kuhlen — told how she stands alone in a weekly silent vigil in Santa Fe, and the powerful impact she believes this has had. Therese Kulugu and Solange Iwashigue Furuha from Women in Black Congo described the effect of the many rapes for which the country is infamous: loss of individual and communal identity, loss of social cohesion, thousands of unwanted children, widespread HIV. They told how one of their hospitals (the Panzi Hospital) was caring for 40,000 rape victims and their 3,000 children, using a holistic medical, psychosocial, legal and economic approach.

Yolanda Aguilar, together with a companion from the *Unión Nacional de Mujeres de Guatemala* (UNAMG), presented a short history of the conflict in Guatemala which is estimated to have caused 200,000 deaths and disappearances. It had occurred mainly between 1960 to 1996 between a dictatorship brought to power by a US-backed military coup and various leftist rebel groups supported chiefly by the ethnic Maya people and the Ladino peasants, who together make up the rural poor of Guatemala. A second military coup in 1982 had brought to power the tyrannical General Efraín Ríos Montt, who was brutal in his pursuit of control, but finally defeated. At the time of the Women in Black *encuentro* in Montevideo, 2013, Ríos Montt was on trial for the crime of sexual enslavement of Mayan women during the armed conflict. Women of Guatemala had contributed a report to the Truth Commission associated with his trial.

The conference ended with a demonstration and vigil accompanied by a ceremony by indigenous Charrúa women who formed a sacred circle with shells they called the spirit of the ancestors. Afterwards, one of the indigenous women stood in front of each of the other women in the circle, saying in Charrúa 'I am part of the whole, as the whole is part me'. A powerful film made by Uruguayan Women in Black was simultaneously projected onto a huge building across the road.

Women in Black in other Latin American countries

Several of the speakers at the XV *encuentro* in Bogotá and the XVI *encuentro* in Montevideo provided information about feminist activism in other Latin American countries. From Chile, for instance, Viviana Muñoz said that women's sexual and reproductive rights were the key issue. The law in Chile criminalises all abortion, including the 'morning after' pill. Several of the Chilean women present at the *encuentro* were currently on trial at home for 'crimes against family order, public morality and moral order'. In response to all this, as well as setting up a 24-hour abortion 'hotline', they had been organising naked protests, in the style of 'Pussy Riot'. Ten thousand people had come to their last demonstration. 'There is a war against women, and we provide the information to give women energy to fight back. The government hates us,' Vivi said, 'that's why we are happy to be here.' [The election of a new President, Gabriel Boric, in 2022 will hopefully mean some changes!].

The Central American Republic of Honduras was represented at the XV *encuentro* in Bogotá by Olga Amparo Sánchez Gómez, who explained that although there was no group in Honduras identifying itself as *Mujeres de Negro*, Honduran women were active in much the same spirit. They were, she said, busy 'creating a counter-culture, a political praxis for ourselves'. They liked to use the term *provocar* — meaning to incite, induce, initiate, provoke laughter — anything that would produce a reaction and induce reflection. She had spoken then of the importance of using the term 'violence against women' rather than 'gender violence'. Abstract terminology, she felt, including the word 'gender', was 'one of the tricks that patriarchy plays to hide the reality of violence against women as people'. Some liked to see 'gender violence' as a public health issue, but she insisted, 'No - it's a *rights* issue.' It need not mean that all women have an identical experience. But violence is a continuous reality in the lives of women. Our bodies have been colonised, Olga said. You had only to think of enforced prostitution, enforced pregnancy, cosmetic surgery.

The only Latin American country apart from Colombia and Uruguay that sustained the practice of Women in Black was Argentina. Nora Morales and two other women who travelled from Argentina to Montevideo for the XVI WIB international conference in 2013 reported that for the previous eighteen months they had been holding an early-evening vigil in the capital, Buenos Aires, on the first Thursday of each month. They had WiB groups elsewhere in Argentina and were aiming to get one in every province. WiB in Argentina, we learned, was 'hosted' by a high-profile group of women known as the *Madres de la Plaza de Mayo*, which had been set up in 1977 to demand the return of the thousands of children and grandchildren who had been 'disappeared' by the regime. The *Madres* also characteristically wore black on their street demonstrations. The repression had started in 1976, enacted by an army trained by the US School of the Americas. 30 per cent of the missing people were women. Some had just vanished, others were known to have been jailed, murdered, raped and forced to have children in concentration camps. Nora talked about the 5,000 individuals still unaccounted for, among whom were her son and grandson. Many of the young children had been 'given' by the government to military families. 'We have found 109 disappeared children so far,' Nora said. 'But it is too little, too few. We have to go on fighting for memory, truth and justice.'

However, by 2019, Marta Sara Pérez, the coordinator of Women in Black in the city of Rosario (MdN Rosario), reported that there was only one group in Argentina that continued 'active in the struggle for human rights and a world that is peaceful, equal and inclusive'. Women in Black had been brought to Rosario through the initiative of Verónica Quenón in 2011. Verónica had been the coordinator of *Mujeres de Negro* Uruguay until she moved to live in Argentina, near Rosario. In Argentina almost 300 women are assassinated annually. That is femicide at the rate of one every 30 hours. On 28 March 2012 Rosario women organised an action they titled 'In your skin', comprising huge graphics making visible gender-based violence, and from this the group of Women in Black in Rosario had formed, coordinated by Marta Sara Pérez. A week later, on 5 April 2012, *Mujeres de Negro Rosario* held the first street action on the corner of Córdoba and Moreno on Saint Martin's

Place, the spot where they continue to mount vigils on the first Thursday of each month, holding placards with the names of murdered women of the province, and regularly tweeting. This group maintains a consistent focus on violence against women. They have developed the capacity to work in the field, supporting, assisting and accompanying women victims of gender violence, and to run workshops to impart to women what they term 'tools of empowerment'.

In recent years they have done a great deal of 'accompanying' of women victims of violence and families of femicide victims. They recount the case of one particular woman, Vanesa Soledad Celma, who happened to be the sister-in-law of Eva Domínguez, a member of *Mujeres de Negro Rosario*. Vanesa was 27 years old, eight months pregnant, and had a five-year-old son. On 29 June 2010, her clothes on fire, she ran out of the house where she had been quarrelling with her partner, Omar Díaz, 37 years old. Soon afterwards she gave birth to her child by emergency caesarean. She died on 22 November 2010, after four months of agony. The court investigation into Vanesa's death was, in the Rosario women's view, deficient. It never considered the gender violence that Vanesa suffered, because she herself never denounced it. It is clear, Rosario WiB say, and should be clear to the Commission for Human Rights at state and international levels, that gender prejudice and a devaluation of women were evident in the way the authorities proceeded. Eva Domínguez formed a group called Families Affected by Femicide with the aim of accompanying family members of femicide victims all the way to the courts in the tortuous process of seeking justice. Sometimes *MdN Rosario* vigils stand facing the Provincial Court of Rosario to challenge the failure of the justice system to protect women's rights.

Apart from *MdN* vigils and 'accompanying' women victims, *MdN Rosario* seek a presence in public politics and in relation to the state, for which they are an active part of the

Consultative Provincial Council for Prevention, Assistance and Eradication of Violence against Women, and of the Consultative Board of the Rosario Municipality. As a collective they are part of the international network of Women in Black, and of PIM, the *Paro Internacional de Mujeres*, or International Women's Strike. At the national level they are part of the National Campaign for the Right to Legal, Safe and Free Abortion. And at the municipal level they are part of the feminist movement of Rosario. In these public sector organisations, the women of *MdN Rosario* aim to intervene in the public sphere to improve or increase what already exists or to create new public policies that allow the deconstruction of patriarchal and masculinist culture and achieve equality of rights so as to be able to construct a society that is inclusive and egalitarian. 'Not one death more!' they proclaim. 'Every death matters!'

Clearly, women in South America have influenced the international Women in Black network in many ways, and at the same time they demonstrate the myriad ways that WiB groups across the world have addressed different forms of violence. The women who first called themselves Women in Black in Israel Palestine cited the *Madres de la Plaza de Mayo* (Mothers of the Plaza Mayo) in Argentina as a key inspiration. Women in Colombia played an important role in the peace negotiations there, and Women in Black Uruguay — living in the aftermath of armed conflict — have focused on challenging femicide and violence against women in the home. This ability to adapt to different situations while connecting them through a theory of the continuum of violence from the fist to the gun, and maintaining international solidarity, has been one of the key features of Women in Black.

NOTES

1   The material here and below attributed to Teresa Aristizabal derives from an interview with her carried out (and translated) by Adriana Medina Lalinde of Women in Black London during a visit to Bogotá in early 2019.

2   The material here and below attributed to Clara Mazo Lopez derives from an interview carried out with her (and translated) by Adriana Medina Lalinde of Women in Black London during a visit to Bogotá in early 2019.

3   The countries were Azerbaijan, Australia, Germany, Austria, Bosnia Herzegovina, Canada, Cyprus, Colombia, Croatia, Denmark, Democratic Republic of Congo, Scotland, Spain, Philippines, France, Italy, India, Israel, Indonesia, Japan, Montenegro, Macedonia, Nepal, Palestine, Switzerland, Sweden, Serbia, Turkey, England, Uruguay and the USA.

4   The material here is drawn from an unpublished document embodying La Ruta Pacifica's invitation to WiB for the XV Encuentro of 2011 in Bogotá.

5   Unpublished report by Sue Finch, London Women in Black, on her return from the XV *encuentro* in Bogotá in 2011.

6   The Black Sash movement in South Africa, a group of white women who protested against discriminatory apartheid laws by holding vigils with a black sash draped over their shoulders between 1955 and 1994

7   Cf mujeresdenegrouruguay.blogspot.com accessed 13 June 2021.

8   The organisations listed are, in addition to these two: *La Comisión Nacional de Seguimiento* (CNS); *Casa de Mujer de la Union; Cotidiano Mujer; Instituto Mujer y Sociedad; Isis Internacional; Lola Press; Mujer Ahora; Mujeres del Sur; Mujeres en Accion; Programa Regional de Formacion en Genero y Politicas Publicas* (FLACSO); *Red de Educacion Popular entre Mujeres* (REPEM; *El Abroja; Foro Juvenil; Unidad Mujer y Desarrollo* (CEPAL); and *Centro Interdisciplinario* (CAMINOS).

9   From an unpublished report by Sue Finch and Liz Khan of London Women in Black on their return from the XVI *encuentro* in Montevideo in 2013.

CHAPTER 7

WOMEN IN BLACK ARMENIA — HOPE FOR THE FUTURE?

As we have seen, Women in Black spread from Israel Palestine to the USA, Italy, former Yugoslavia, the UK, Spain, Belgium, India, South Africa, South and Central America and beyond. There are also active groups in Austria, Canada, Denmark, France, Germany, the Netherlands, Australia and many more countries. This chapter looks at one of the most recent Women in Black groups — Armenia — perhaps the hope for the future?

WiB Armenia was founded in 2011, with the support of the Society Without Violence NGO, and first appeared at an international conference in Uruguay in 2013. They brought with them a new wave of activism that was courageous and fun, with a film showing huge numbers of young WiB in a flash mob dance in the central square of the capital of Armenia, Yerevan. This built on work they had been involved in with schools, colleges and universities — in the face of terrible and ongoing border wars.

Armenia is one of the most ancient countries in the world. The name appears in the earliest map on a clay tablet from the 6th century BCE in the British Museum; later it developed into a vast empire. Literacy came earlier than in Europe. Christianity was adopted as the state religion in 301 CE. As a Christian kingdom set among warring neighbours, Armenia was an East-West trading crossroads. A constellation of principalities, its borders changed over time. During the Middle Ages, crusading European armies rested there. Armenian arts and culture absorbed influences from East and West with striking individuality and finesse in architecture, metal work, jewellery, manuscript illumination, sculpture, music, ceramics, carpets and textiles. Women played an important role, both in the Christianisation of Armenia and as rulers who contributed to the cultural and socio-economic development of Armenia.

Greater Armenia was ruled in the East by Persia, while the expansion of the Ottoman Empire brought Western Armenia under the Ottoman protectorate. Armenians were defined by their religion, subjected to heavy taxation, persecution and discrimination, with inferior status under Muslim law. Fear of rape, abduction and enforced marriages or servitude compelled women to lead sequestered lives during the centuries of Ottoman domination.

Massacres in Armenian towns and villages by Turks took place periodically under the Ottoman occupation. In 1915 the Young Turks implemented a meticulously planned attack on Armenian citizens, killing and torturing the men, forcing families to march across the country to the deserts of Syria, and taking possession of Armenian homes, goods and lands. Estimates of more than two and half million killed and millions dispossessed during this genocide are still denied by Turkey.

The efforts of Armenians to hold on to the fertile mountainous region of Karabagh were opposed by the British, who controlled the area after 1918 and gave it to Azerbaijan, to secure control of Baku oil, on 15 January 1919. Armenia, Azerbaijan and Georgia were absorbed by the Soviet regime in the 1920s, and Armenia became a Republic of the USSR, reduced to a miniscule fraction (1/32) of its former territory. Nonetheless it became a powerhouse for science and computer technology.

The disputed territory of Nagorno Karabagh, or Artsakh to Armenians, had been settled by Armenians since the seventh century BCE, with ancient citadels, bridges and churches, a treasure trove of 4,000 historic sites: cities, churches, castles, fortresses, bridges — all inscribed with ancient Armenian script.

Nearby Nakhchivan had become part of Azerbaijan in 1921, as part of the Treaty of Moscow between Soviet Russia and Turkey. Armenian cultural monuments and churches were destroyed; many Armenians feared that the same fate might befall Karabagh.

After Armenia's independence from the USSR in 1991, Karabagh declared self-government but remained an unrecognised state. In the post-Soviet power vacuum, military action between Azerbaijan and Armenia saw thousands of soldiers and civilians killed and people displaced on both sides. Fighting continued, culminating in the 2020 war during which Azerbaijan attacked Karabagh with drones, missiles and cluster bombs, burning towns, villages and forests. The international community remained largely indifferent. A ceasefire was finally brokered, and a Russian peacekeeping force sent to patrol borders.

An estimated 75,000 Armenians were displaced from Karabagh in 2020, most of them women and children. Over 4,000 troops were killed on each side of the conflict, as were hundreds of civilians. Unlike refugees in war zones, 'people fleeing from war in internationally unrecognized states do not have sufficient protection under International Law' writes UN expert in trafficking and slavery, Gulnara Shahinian.[1] The brutality and injustice of the 1915 genocide was evoked again.

Women in Black Armenia, an antimilitarist, feminist, peace-building initiative founded by eleven young women from different regions of Armenia, formed a rapid response group to support the refugees alongside their peacekeeping activities. WiB organise conflict resolution training in schools, movie screenings, discussions related to peacebuilding and women's involvement in peacebuilding and decision-making processes, public actions like flash-mob singing and dancing, and peace camps.[2]

FiLiA interviewed WiB Armenia in January 2021 about the 2020 war, and their vision for the future:

Women In Black Armenia Speak Out (FiLiA 29.1.21)[3]

Women in Black Armenia, Sona Hovakimyan and Arpi Balyan share their opinions and thoughts about the 2020 Nagorno-Karabakh war which began on 27 September 2020 and lasted 44 days. The war ended after three failed ceasefires on 9 November 2020, when Armenia, Azerbaijan and Russia signed an agreement to end the military conflict. This is the first of FILIA's Women in Black series, a powerful collection of testimonies from women peace activists from across the globe.

Dear Sisters,

Nowadays it is hard to speak about how we live today and how we feel about the situation in our country, but we will try to sum up and share some insights about what we do, and what has been done during these days. Our speech may be too emotional, but this is a kind of resistance voice against expansionism, colonialism and brutal war.

Let's start with a brief introduction to Women in Black Armenia initiative. The vision of Women in Black Armenia peacebuilding initiative is to have a society where law and human rights prevail, conflicts are regulated in a peaceful manner, women are actively involved in peacebuilding and decision-making processes at all levels, and there is no space for violence.

Thus, the mission of the group is to promote the ideology of peace, to direct young women to spread democratic values in the Republic of Armenia, to involve women in civic initiatives, as well as in peacebuilding procedures at all levels.

We were very excited to organise a Women in Black international gathering in Armenia in 2021, but it has been very challenging, not only during the pandemic but also during the war we are still living in since 27

September 2020, and which is an imminent threat to our existence. We cannot give detailed and full information about what led to this outbreak of the conflict, but we can outline some facts and conclusions.

First of all, it is obvious that the main militaristic actions have been started by Azerbaijani militarist and political authorities, with the help of the Turkish expansionist government. This is not a subject of argument, and it is clear that a small and economically poor country wouldn't initiate this war. Besides, this was the result of lasting hatred, aggression and miscommunication between two nations, exacerbated by the dictatorship of Aberzaijani President Aliyev. This was a result of failed diplomacy between Armenia and Azerbaijan.

We couldn't reach for solidarity on both sides, and save stability in our region, because we were not able to see the whole picture of expansionism and colonialism by Turkey and Russia and play a significant role in ongoing political processes. All antimilitarist and feminist future is uncertain now. One thing that we can do now is to learn lessons from our failures.

During the war more than 75,000 people were displaced from Artsakh to Armenia. Most of them lost their loved ones, their homes, their properties to the war. There is a huge need for assisting displaced people from Artsakh to Armenia since September 27th 2020, by providing them with food, shelter and basic necessities, women who can protect, as well as Covid-19 prevention measures. We are providing humanitarian assistance to displaced families living in Yerevan, and in regions of Armenia. In addition, we have formed a rapid response group consisting of members of Women in Black Armenia, which deals with the needs of families left without any support, providing them with the necessary assistance, including psychological support. Sending love solidarity and peace. (FiLiA newsletter 29.1.2021)

Two further interviews with Armenian Women in Black Arpi Balyan and Sonia Hovakimyane in Armenia took place by zoom with Sue Finch from WiB London in May 2021.

Many Armenian women were attracted to WiB because of its feminist, international and antimilitarist vision, particularly in the light of their own history. Key themes from the interviews were a focus on educating young women, feminist values and connecting across borders.

Educating for peace

Educating young women about feminism and peace is a central theme for WiB Armenia activists. Arpi became part of WiB in 2014, and rapidly started organising feminist peacebuilding workshops with young women and girls:

> I was 23 years old in 2014 and at that period looking for groups who were actively involved in the feminist movement, when I went to a workshop led by a woman who was part of the Women in Black initiative. She was talking about gender equality, women's rights, and the WiB Armenia peacebuilding initiative. After the workshop she gave us her contact details, and I became part of WiB. I was searching for feminist justice, because that period was hard for me; patriarchal, hetero-normal society is very cruel to women. There are a lot of family pressures for heterosexual relationships in my family and this conservative society. In Women in Black Armenia, I found values which are relevant to my values. It became the start of my peacebuilding activism.

> We started to organise a lot of workshops with young Armenian women and girls: this was very educational for me. I couldn't imagine where this path would lead

us, and Women in Black: I've been involved in so many educational programmes about feminism, peacebuilding, antimilitarism and the dangers of nationalist extremism and fascism.

Sonya was studying and working for an NGO when she heard about WiB, and began to organise training on women's rights and gender equality in schools, and feminist peace camps for young women:

> When I heard about Women in Black, I had been searching for a long time to do something in this sphere. As a social worker by profession, now studying psychology for a Master's degree, I consider myself a humanist, helping people — so I want to bring about positive changes for peace: this is close to my heart. I realised WiB was where I wanted to be, to bring peace to people — part of my mission in the world — that's why I joined WiB.
>
> I had been working as part of an NGO, Societies Without Violence, in a women's rights project, but we have become a separate, independent organisation as Women in Black. We provide peacebuilding training on women's rights and gender equality, and feminist peace camps for young women (16-25) where they can share their thoughts, as well as offering safe places and space for them. We work in schools and have an office in Yerevan where we hold gatherings and courses. Because of the pandemic, we have virtual meetings as well.

Art for peace

There is also a strong emphasis on art for peace in Armenian WiB, as Arpi describes:

> I launched an antimilitarist arts project, with lots of exhibitions of graphic art in Yerevan, the capital; Abovyan — my hometown; Gyumri and Vanadzor; the biggest cities in Armenia. Women in Black

Armenia helped me so much with this. There are a few feminist artists in Armenia — but feminism is seen as 'problematic', we are met with hostility. I know a lot of artists who avoid the term 'feminist', because of sexism and misogyny.

It is difficult for us to travel, if you don't have any funding, Armenia is one of the poorest countries in the world, and the political situation is very uncertain.

Up until 2015-16 we were dancing for peace in the main street of Yerevan, and the main square, we created WiB flash mobs — but after that things got more difficult because of hostility from men. Since the last war (with Azerbaijan in 2020), hostility has been growing, people are getting more hostile as nationalism and militarism are on the rise. The pressures on us are growing. Now we have an office, and we operate through small workshops. We don't hold vigils: it doesn't feel safe.

Sonya added:

Dancing was a big part of our Women in Black campaigns at first — on the streets, in the squares, in flash mobs — but nowadays, with the political situation after the last war (in 2020), there is less tolerance for what are seen as 'European values', and a more aggressive attitude towards us. So it's harder for us to organise public activities.

We try to work more on peacebuilding with young women now, about values, changing people's hearts. They don't need aggression and hate, it damages everyone. No matter where I'm working — some years ago I worked in prisons with male prisoners — for me it's the same thing: men need to change as much as women. This is the core of my vision for peacebuilding.

Feminist values

Arpi is clear that feminist values are central to all their peace-building work in WiB Armenia:

> The most important aspect of Women in Black for me is that it is based on feminist values — the ties of sisterhood are very strong. WiB is spread all over the world, we connect with zoom, we share problems, we rebel together, and we help each other. In Armenia, we meet regularly, and we implement strong feminist programmes: workshops and peace camps for young women and girls.
>
> We also have friends who translate feminist texts into Armenian and have started a book group where we read these translations … there are very few feminist books written by Armenian women or translated into Armenian. Right now we are reading Sara Ahmed, *Living a Feminist Life*. Maybe in a couple of years I'll write my own book!
>
> I work with WiB Armenia and at the Feminist Library in Yerevan, where we have collected lots of feminist and other books, mostly in English, but also in German, Russian and French and a few in Armenian. But I have learned more in WiB activism about gender equality and women's rights than I could from studying.

Sonya added that there is a new generation of Armenian women coming through who are ready to claim their rights:

> We are building a network where young women can connect with us if they want to take part in self-help groups or arts exhibitions and projects. We try to encourage them to speak up, engage with feminist issues, and be strong and change their lives. This is a very patriarchal society, with the usual gender-based stereotypes, and violence against women. Women are

not treated equally, and face not only gender stereotypes and physical violence but also psychological and economic violence, especially in the regions and villages. But the new generation of young women is more aware of their rights and ready to claim them. We help women to change their lives.

It's not easy work, but very empowering — when you reach someone, and you see the changes in them, it gives you more energy! We meet a lot, we discuss, share emotions and thoughts, and support each other. In this world, we need each other. Women in Black is something I can lean on, I can trust. It's an opportunity to bring about some changes to the world, to bring peace and love to people.

Connecting across borders

In the aftermath of the recent wars between Azerbaijan and Armenia, Sonya describes the importance of connecting across borders:

The whole world is important for us — we are all connected. We are all one, even if we are separated by borders and nations. Deep inside we are all the same. We don't want to build enemies outside of our country or ourselves — at a national level some people do, but if you hate you don't help anyone. Aggressors and abusers need to change, but peacebuilding needs to do it with love in the structure.

Nothing will work if you are not doing it with healing — ideas don't change people without love. If you build barriers — 'they are not one of us' or 'they are perpetrators' — it doesn't help. People do bad/aggressive things, and it can be very difficult, there can be obstacles to overcome, but there are also tools that can help change the world. If you see people as 'the other side', you will not be able to change anything, that's the end of all activity. Understanding people is very important, understanding that aggression needs healing.

The Armenian WiB focus on educating young women for peace and through art, feminist values, connecting across borders, and healing were all guiding themes for the WiB conference they hosted in 2021.

XVIII WiB international conference in 2021

At the Women in Black conference in South Africa in 2018, WiB Armenia had taken on the task of organising the next international conference in 2020. The conference was delayed by the outbreak of the Covid pandemic that year, and then by the ongoing war between Azerbaijan and Armenia. This was very difficult for WiB Armenia, who had booked hotels and venues in 2020, and raised money for women from the Global South to attend. They eventually organised the first international WiB conference to be held on zoom, in 2021.

Conference participants included women from Afghanistan, Argentina, Armenia, Belgium, Cameroon, Germany, India, Israel, the Kakuma refugee camp in Kenya, Serbia, South Africa, Spain, UK, US and Uruguay.

Mariam Mughdusyan from Armenia opened the conference by describing the current crisis with Azerbaijan, which had displaced many Armenians living in Ngorno-Karabagh in 2020, and the wider challenges faced by WiB Armenia. In addition to campaigning for peace, Women in Black Armenia were providing free education for refugee children and had opened a social enterprise arts centre, community restaurant and shop selling art and embroidery to help fund and promote their work.

Another Armenian WiB, Mariam Egiazaryan described the impact of the war in Ngorno-Karabagh on the environment, working in dialogue with Azerbaijani researchers. The Conflict and Environment Observatory (a UK organisation that aims to understand the effects of war on the environment) found that there were over twice as many forest fires in Ngorno-Karabagh in 2020 as in the eight previous years put together, destroying 1,815 hectares of forest.

Heena Thompson from WiB UK added that the Women's International League for Peace and Freedom, Extinction Rebellion and Stop Ecocide organisations are campaigning for an international law on ecocide, defined as: 'unlawful or wanton acts committed with knowledge that there is a substantial likelihood of severe and widespread or long-term damage to the environment being caused by those acts' (Haroon Siddique, *Guardian* 22.6.2021).

Heena also campaigns to support women from the Kakuma refugee camp in Kenya, who talked at the conference about the terrible conditions they were living in, isolated as lesbians in one block with their children, raped and assaulted by the guards, waiting indefinitely for decisions about their future.

Knar Khudoyan from Armenia described spending the 2020 war in isolation, and its effects on mental health. Vita Arrufat from Valencia and Yvonne Deutsch from Israel led sessions on self-care and community well-being in times of trauma. Bernedette Muthien from South Africa spoke about Indigenous Women's Wisdoms for healing from Southern Africa.

The conference in July 2021 was groundbreaking in many ways. There was a new focus on the disastrous effects of war on the environment as well as on people, and on the importance of women peace activists taking care of their own mental and physical health to avoid burn-out, supporting each other and keeping hope alive for the future.

> We have to learn to deal with things without losing our positive attitudes, our hope, our love, our light. This is the hardest part, but the amazing and empowering part as well! Then you can feel the support of each other, and the strength not to lose your mind in this chaos, this bad situation your country or the world is facing. There is always hope. We should not give up — we should

see things from a bigger perspective. Change is going
on — if we lose our hope, then who will do our work?
How can we change anything? (Sonya Hovakimyane
interview with Sue Finch 17.5.2021)

NOTES

1   Armenian diplomat and author Shahinian is a member of the Group of
    Experts on Action Against Trafficking in Human Beings and the former
    UN Special Rapporteur on Contemporary Forms of Slavery (2006 -
    2014)
2   https://womeninblackarmenia.weebly.com/ (accessed 24 June 2021)
3   https://filia.org.uk/ interviews in FiLiA newsletter (accessed 24 June
    2021). FiLiA is an international women-led volunteer organisation
    based in the UK and part of the Women's Liberation Movement.
    FiLiA means daughter. FiLiA's vision is a world free from patriarchy
    where all women and girls are liberated: 'we are the daughters of
    the women who came before us and we fight so that our sisters and
    daughters may be free'.

AFTERWORD

For a network held together by shared passion and aims, with no membership or organisational structure, Women in Black has reached surprisingly far and wide in just over thirty years.

As we have seen, starting with Israeli and Palestinian women taking a stand against the occupation of Palestine, subsequently taken to what was then Yugoslavia by Italian women, and spreading from there to the UK, Spain, Belgium, India, South Africa, North and South America, Armenia and beyond, Women in Black continue to campaign with imagination and determination for peace and justice.

Many different WiB groups act against the continuum of violence that flows in both directions from rape and murder in war to the murder and rape of women in the home. Some, working within occupation or war zones, focus mainly on peace with justice. Others campaign against violence against women in the home, and for justice for women. Most do both, and all are connected.

Each group has developed its own priorities and ways of working, constantly evolving in response to local and international challenges, conflicts and violence. Connecting with each other across borders to find ways to negotiate and end conflicts, organising dramatic non-violent actions and demonstrations of up to 30,000 people, and sustaining vigils — even when they are just one person — Women in Black have developed and share a feminist understanding that current gender power relations predispose societies to violence and war.

Women use drama, ritual and symbolism (choosing to wear black, the colour of mourning in many cultures), silence or rhyme, rhythm and music depending on their cultures, learning from each other across borders to turn protests against militarism and male violence into creative experiences of their opposites. The Courts of Women developed in India by Corinne Kumar take this further, hearing personal testimonies of crimes against women interwoven with drama, dance, and poetry, calling for justice for women and seeking redress and reparations.

These new ways of working depend on close partnerships with other feminist movements in each country, building on shared strengths and developing joint actions.

The international, antimilitarist feminisms of Women in Black are based on a critique of capitalism and imperialism, the main motors of militarism and war. They bring together women across cultures, religions and ethnicities with a shared analysis of gender relations, and how these intersect.

WiB protests have developed to include the displacement of refugees, asylum seekers, and enslaved peoples. They connect spending on nuclear weapons and militarism to the rapidly growing impact of environmental catastrophe.

Standing on the shoulders of many others, like the Women's International League for Peace and Freedom, *Vimochana* in India, *Ruta Pacifica* in Colombia, Greenham Common peace women in the UK, and many more, Women in Black aims to defend international human rights and women's rights by campaigning for peace with justice.

It may be too soon to say with any confidence, but it seems clear that Women in Black has grown beyond a network. Could it be a movement?

If so, there may be some hope for the future.

BIBLIOGRAPHY

Amnesty International (2017) *Wounds That Burn Our Souls, Compensation For Kosovo's Wartime Rape Survivors, But Still No Justice* https://www.amnesty.org/download/Documents/ EUR7075582017ENGLISH.PDF (accessed 19.7.2021).

Augustin, Ebba (1993) 'Preface', in Ebba Augustin (ed.) *Palestinian Women: Identity and Experience*. Zed Books, London and New Jersey.

Bertell, Rosalie (1985) *No Immediate Danger: Prognosis for a Radioactive Earth*, The Women's Press, London.

Bracewell, Wendy (1996) 'Women, Motherhood and Contemporary Serbian Nationalism', *Women's Studies International Forum*, No.19 (1/2), pp. 25-33.

Braunw, Esther et al (1984), *Mujer, Paz y Militarismo*. Madrid: *Fundación de Investigaciones Marxistas*.

Caldicott, Dr Helen, (1986), *Missile Envy: The Arms Race and Nuclear War*, Bantam Doubleday Dell Publishing Group.

Cantor, Aviva (1990) 'A Brief Guide to the Jewish Community', in *Jewish Women's Call for Peace: A Handbook for Jewish Women on the Israeli/Palestinian Conflict*, Firebrand Books, Ithaca, New York.

Casa delle Donne Torino (1994) 'The Italian Case: An Open Experience', unpublished paper, authored by Luisa Corbetta, Elisabetta Donini, Anna Garelli, Margherita Granero and Carla Ortona. Turin, Italy.

Chazan, Naomi (1993) 'Israeli women and peace activism', in Swirski, Barbara and Marilyn P. Safir (eds) *Calling the Equality Bluff: Women in Israel*. Athene Series, Teachers College Press, New York and London.

Cockburn, Cynthia (1998) *The Space Between Us: Negotiating Gender and National Identities in Conflict* London: Zed Books. ISBN: 1 85649 617 1 hardback, 1 85649 617 x paperback.

— Published in Russian as Prostranstvo mezhdu nami: Obsuzhdenie gendemykh I natsional'nykh identichnostiej v konfliktakh. Perevod:

M.Torkhshoievoi. 2002. Moskva: Idieja-Press ISBN 5-7333-0055-8.
— Published in Turkish as Mesafeyi Asmak: Baris Mucadelesinde
Kadinlar. Istanbul: Iletisim Yayinlari. 2004. ISBN 975-05-0212-4.
— Published in Japanese as Funso ka no jennda- to esunisity; nashinaru
aidenntiti o koete, Akashi Shoten, Tokyo. 2004. ISBN 4-7503-1998-
8.
— Also published in Georgian 2002, ISBN 99928-45-96-1, Serbo-
Croat 2003, ISBN 953 99298-0-6, Bulgarian, and Japanese ISBN
4-7503-1998-8 CO336.
Cockburn, Cynthia and Lynette Hunter (1999) 'Transversal politics
and translating practices', Soundings: A Journal of Politics and
Culture, Issue 12, Summer.
Cockburn Cynthia (2001) Women Organizing for Change: A study of
women's local integrative organizations in the pursuit of democracy
in Bosnia-Herzegovina. (Co-authored with Meliha Hubic and Rada
Stakic-Domuz) Published by Medica Women's Association, Bosnia,
and the Open Society Institute, ISBN 9958-9586-8-6 and 9 789958
958687. Published in Bosnian language as Zivjeti Zajedno Ili Zivjeti
Odvojeno. Drugli Pogled series No.5, Zenica, June 2001.
Cockburn Cynthia (2002) The Postwar Moment: Militaries, Masculinities
and International Peacekeeping. (Co-edited with Dubravka Zarkov),
London: Lawrence and Wishart. ISBN: 0-85315-946-7
Cockburn Cynthia (2004) The Line: Women, Partition and the Gender
Order in Cyprus. London and New York: Zed Books ISBN 1 84277
420 4 and 421 2.
— Published in Turkish as Hat: Kibrista Kadinlar, Taksim ve Toplumsal
Cinsiyet Duzeni. Istanbul: Iletisim. 2005. ISBN 975 05 0375 9.
— Published in Greek by Metaixmio, Athens. 2006. ISBN 978-960-
455- 306-8
Cockburn, Cynthia (2005) Violence as indivisible: Women in Black,
Vimochana and the Asian Women's Human Rights Council,
Bangalore, India, unpublished Research Profile No.11, 7 April 2005.
Cockburn Cynthia (2007) From Where We Stand: War, Women's
Activism and Feminist Analysis. London and New York: Zed Books.
ISBN 978 1 84277 821 0 paperback, and 820 3 hardback.
— Published in Spanish as Mujeres ante la Guerra: Desde Donde
Estamos. Barcelona: Icaria. 2007. ISBN 978-84-9888-073-1.
— Published in Turkish as Buradan Baktigimizda: Kadinlarin
Militarizme Karsi Mucadelesi. 2009. Istanbul: Metis Yayinlari.
— Published in Korean by Sam In Publishers, Seoul. 2009. ISBN 978-
89- 6436-001-9.

Cockburn, Cynthia (2010) *Gender Relations as Causal in Militarisation and War – A Feminist Standpoint*, International Feminist Journal of Politics 12:2 June

Cockburn, Cynthia (September 2010) *Women-against-NATO: Making a Feminist Case*, Broken Rifle No.86

Cockburn, Cynthia (24/11/2010) *N-A-T-O, What's that stand for?* openDemocracy 50.50 https://www.opendemocracy.net/en/5050/n-a-t-o-whats-that-stand-for/ (accessed 15.6.2021)

Cockburn, Cynthia (2012) *Antimilitarism: Political and Gender Dynamics of Peace Movements*, Basingstoke, UK, and New York: Palgrave Macmillan. ISBN 978-0-230-35974-1 (hardback) and 978-0-230-35975-8 (paperback).

— Published in Catalan by *Institut Català Internacional per la Pau*, Barcelona, Cataluna, Spain, as *Antimilitarisme: Dinàmiques Polítiques I de Gènere dels Moviments per la Pau*. Pròleg de Carme Alemany. 2014. ISBN 978-84-9975-535-9

Cockburn, Cynthia (25.11.2012) *Don't talk to me about war. My life's a battlefield.* openDemocracy 50.50

Cockburn, Cynthia (2013) *War and security, women and gender: an overview of the issues*, Gender & Development, 21:3, 433-52, DOI: 10.1080/13552074.2013.846632

Cockburn, Cynthia (2015) *Des Femmes contre le Militarisme et la Guerre* La Dispute, Paris. Translated by Severine Sofio, preface by Arielle Denis.ISBN 978-2-84303-252-3.

Cockburn, Cynthia (30.4.2015) *World disarmament? Start by disarming masculinity*, openDemocracy 50.50

Cockburn Cynthia, (2017) *Looking to London: Stories of War, Escape and Asylum*. London: Pluto Press. ISBN 978-0-7453-9922-5 (hardback) and 978-0-7453- 9921-8 (paperback).

Cohen, Esther (1990) 'New York: Women on the Road to Peace', in *Jewish Women's Call for Peace: A Handbook for Jewish Women on the Israeli/Palestinian Conflict*, Rita Falbel (Editor), Firebrand Books, Ithaca, New York

Coordinating Committee of the Jewish Women's Committee to End the Occupation (1990) 'Introduction', in *Jewish Women's Call for Peace: A Handbook for Jewish Women on the Israeli/Palestinian Conflict*, Rita Falbel (Editor), Firebrand Books, Ithaca, New York.

Davis, Uri (1987) *Israel: An Apartheid State*. Zed Books, London and New Jersey.

Deutsch, Yvonne (1994) 'Israeli women against the Occupation: political growth and the persistence of ideology' in Tamar Mayer (ed) *Women and the Israeli Occupation: The Politics of Change*. Routledge, New York.

Drakulić, Slavenka (1993) 'Women and the New Democracy in the Former Yugoslavia', in Fund, Nanette and Magda Mueller (eds) *Gender Politics and Post-Communism*. Routledge, London and New York.

Enloe, Cynthia (1989) *Bananas, Beaches and Bases - Making feminist sense of international politics*, Pandora Press, Ontario, Canada.

Espanioli, Nabila (1993) 'Palestinian Women in Israel respond to the Intifada', in Svirski, Barbara and Marilyn P.Safir (eds) *Calling the Equality Bluff: Women in Israel*. Athene Series, Teachers College Press, Columbia University, New York and London.

Espanioli, Nabila (1994) 'Palestinian Women in Israel: Identity in Light of the Occupation', in Mayer, Tamar (ed) *Women and the Israeli Occupation*. Routledge, London and New York.

Falbel, Rita (1990) 'Women's Vigil Against the Occupation', *Jewish Women's Call for Peace: A Handbook for Jewish Women on the Israeli/Palestinian Conflict*. Firebrand Books, Ithaca, New York.

Feminism and Non-Violence Study Group, *Piecing It Together: Feminism and Nonviolence (1983), published by War Resisters International*, 2010 https://wri-irg.org/en/story/2010/piecing-it-together-feminism-and-nonviolence (accessed 7.8.2021)

Golan, Galia (1995) 'Women in Israeli Society: An Overview', in *Palestine-Israel Journal of Politics, Economics and Culture*, Vol.II, No.3, Jerusalem, Israel.

González, Fernán E. (2004) 'Alternatives to War: Colombia's Peace Processes', in *Accord: International Review of Peace Initiatives*, Issue No.14, Conciliation Resources, London.

Gorelick, Sherry (1991) 'Geneva Conference', in *Bridges*, Vol.2, No.2, Fall. Bridges Association, online at < https://www.jstor.org/publisher/bridgesassoc> (accessed 9.11.2021)

Grossman, David (1993) *Sleeping on a Wire: Conversations with Palestinians in Israel*. Picador/Pan Macmillan, London and Basingstoke.

Hood, Laura (2021) 'Colombia's Fragile Peace Deal Threatened by the Return of Mass Killings' 15 February 2021 in *The Conversation*. Online at https//theconversation.com/colombias-fragile-peace-deal-threatened-by-the-return-of-mass-killings-154315 (accessed 16.6.2021)

Human Rights Watch (2021) *World Report, Colombia, 2021*. Online at https://www.hrw.org/world-report/2021/country-chapters/colombia (accessed16.6.21).

Jaffe, Sharon (1990) 'Minneapolis: A Report on the Hannah Arendt Lesbian Peace Patrol', in *Jewish Women's Call for Peace: A Handbook for Jewish Women on the Israeli/Palestinian Conflict.* Firebrand Books, Ithaca, New York.

Johnson, Rebecca (2016) '*World Courts of Women: Against War, For Peace*', openDemocracy 50.50 Online Journal, https://www.opendemocracy.net/en/5050/courts-of-women-resisting-violence-and-war/ (accessed 9.11.2021)

Kinberg, Clare (1990) 'American Jewish Hopes and Fears', in *Jewish Women's Call for Peace: A Handbook for Jewish Women on the Israeli/Palestinian Conflict.* Ed. Rita Falbel, Firebrand Books, Ithaca, New York.

Klepfisz, Irena (1990) 'Yom Hashoah, Yom Yerushalayim: A Meditation' in *Jewish Women's Call for Peace: A Handbook for Jewish Women on the Israeli/Palestinian Conflict.* Ed. Rital Farbel, Firebrand Books, Ithaca, New York.

Kumar, Corinne (2015) *World Court of Women against War, for Peace.* Booklet produced to accompany the Court held at Mount Carmel College, Bangalore, India, 16 November 2015.

Laqueur, Walter (2003) *The History of Zionism.* Weidenfeld and Nicolson, London.

Lerner, Gerda (1986) *The Creation of Patriarchy,* Oxford University Press

Magaš, Branka (1993) *The Destruction of Yugoslavia: Tracking the Break-up of 1980-92.* Verso: London and New York.

Manchanda et al (2002) *Women Making Peace: Strengthening Women's Role in Peace Processes,* booklet, Kathmandu: South Asia Forum for Human Rights

Meertens, Donny (2001) 'The Nostalgic Future: Terror, Displacement and Gender in Colombia', in Moser, Caroline O.N. and Fiona C.Clark (eds) *Victims, Perpetrators or Actors? Gender, Armed Conflict and Political Violence.* London and New York: Zed Books.

Miškovska Kajevska, Ana (2017) *Feminist Activism at War: Belgrade and Zagreb Feminists in the 1990s.* London: Routledge. Online resource at the British Library, accessed March 2019.

MOC (Movimiento de Objeción de Conciencia) (2002) *En Legítima Desobediencia: Tres Décadas de Objeción, Insumisión y Antimilitarismo.* Published in Madrid by *Movimiento de Objeción de Conciencia,* with *El Proyecto Editorial Traficantes de Sueños.*

Morokvasić, Mirjana (1986) 'Being a Woman in Yugoslavia: Past, Present and Institutional Equality', in Godantt, Monique (ed) *Women of the Mediterranean.* Zed Books, London.

Nevel, Donna (1990) 'Jewish Women's Call for Peace — Days of Awe' in *Jewish Women's Call for Peace: A Handbook for Jewish Women on the Israeli/Palestinian Conflict*. Ed. Rita Farbel, Firebrand Books, Ithaca, New York.

Orr, Akiva (1994) *Israel: Politics, Myths and Identity Crises*. Pluto Press, London and Boulder, Colorado.

Oz, Amos (1994) *Israel, Palestine and Peace. Essays*. Vintage, London.

Pappé, Ilan (2006) *The Ethnic Cleansing of Palestine*. One World Publishers, Oxford.

Peleg, Ilan and Dov Waxman (2011) *Israel's Palestinians: The Conflict Within*. Cambridge University Press, Cambridge.

Safran, Hannah (2005) 'Alliance and Denial: Lesbian Protest in Women in Black', in Shadmi, Erella and Chava Frankfort-Nachmias (eds.), *Sappho in the Holy Land: Lesbian Existence and Dilemmas in Contemporary Israel*. SUNY Press, New York.

Shadmi, Erella (2000) 'Between Resistance and Compliance, Feminism and Nationalism: Women in Black, Israel', in *Women's Studies International Forum*, Vol.23, No.1.

Shadmi, Erella (2004) 'Back to Womanhood: Feminism in Globalised Israel'. Unpublished paper, presented to the UK Women's Studies Conference on Feminism Contesting Globalization, at University College Dublin, July 8-10, 2004.

Sharoni, Simona (1994) 'Homefront as Battlefield: Gender, Military Occupation and Violence against Women', in Mayer, Tamar (ed) *Women and the Israeli Occupation*. Routledge, London and New York.

Sharoni, Simona (1995) *Gender and the Israeli-Palestinian Conflict: The Politics of Women's Resistance*. Syracuse University Press, New York.

Silber, Laura and Allan Little (1995) *The Death of Yugoslavia*. Penguin Books, London and New York.

Svirsky, Gila (1996) *Standing for Peace: A History of Women in Black in Israel*, online at <http://www.gilasvirsky.com/wib_book.html> (accessed 14.6.2021)

Rodriguez, Jorge Rojas (2004) 'Political Peacebuilding: A Challenge for Civil Society', in Garcia-Duran, Mauricio (ed), Alternatives to War: Colombia's Peace Processes, in *Accord: International Review of Peace Initiatives*, Issue No.14, Conciliation Resources.

'Ruta Pacífica de las Mujeres', Carla Afonso and Carlos Martín Beristain (2013) *Memoria Para La Vida: Una Comisión de la Verdad desde las Mujeres para Colombia*. Bilbao, Spain: Universidad del País Vasco and Hegoa.

UN Women (2015) 'Preventing conflict, transforming justice, securing the peace' — A Global Study on the Implementation of United Nations Security Council Resolution 1325 https://wps.unwomen.org/ (accessed 16.6.2021)

Treaty on the Prohibition of Nuclear Weapons, online at https://undocs.org/A/CONF.229/2017/8 (accessed 15.6.2021)

VLD - Visitare Luoghi Difficile (1988) Visitare Luoghi Difficile: 2, unpublished paper authored by the three participating groups: Casa delle Donne di Torino, Donne Dell'Associazione per la Pace and the Centro Delle Donne di Bologna. Referred to in the text as VLD 1988.

VLD (1992) Visitare Luoghi Difficili, 'An Experience of Sponsorship of Palestinian Little Girls'. September. Unpublished paper. Authored by the Casa Delle Donne di Torino.

VLD (1994) Visitare Luoghi Difficili, Adoption Programme in the Gaza Strip and West Bank: A Joint Study Evaluating the Child Adoption Programme in Palestine. Unpublished paper authored by the Casa delle Donne, Torino, Italy, with Women's Affairs Gaza, Women's Affairs Nablus and Women's Studies Centre, Jerusalem.

White, Ben (2012) Palestinians in Israel: Segregation, Discrimination and Democracy. Pluto Press, London and New York.

WILPF Statement: International Women's Day for Peace and Disarmament 2021 https://www.wilpf.org/wp-content/uploads/2021/05/English-IWD-for-Peace-and-Disarmament-Statement.pdf (accessed 16 June 2021)

WOMEN SAY 'NO TO NATO' statement 20 November 2010, online http://www.wloe.org/London-20-Nov-2010.586.0.html (accessed 16.6.2021)

Woodward, Susan L. (1995) Balkan Tragedy: Chaos and Dissolution after the Cold War. Brookings Institution: Washington.

Yuval-Davis, Nira (1997) Gender and Nation, Sage Publications: London and Thousand Oaks, New Delhi.

Zamarra, Cthuchi (2009) 'Conscientious Objection in Spain: Disobedience', in Özgür Heval Çinar and Coskun Üsterci (eds), Resisting Militarized Society: Conscientious Objection. Zed Books London and New York.

ŽuC (1993, 1994, 1997, 1998, 1999, 2001, 2007) Žene u Crnom Protiv Rata. Successive issues of the annual volume Women for Peace, written and published by Žene u Crnom Protiv Rata, Belgrade.

www.womeninblack.org

INDEX OF ORGANISATIONS

Women in Black groups

ARGENTINA
Mujeres de Negro

Buenos Aires
Email: mujeresdenegroargentina@hotmail.com.ar

Rosario
Email: mujeresdenegrorosario@gmail.com
Twitter: @MdNArgentina
skype: mujeresdenegro.argentina

ARMENIA

Facebook: https://www.facebook.com/womeninblackarmenia
Twitter: Follow us @arm_wib
Blog: http://womeninblackarmenia.weebly.com/
Email: arm.womeninblack@gmail.com

AUSTRALIA

Melbourne
Email: Joan Nestle Joan.jessbsimple@gmail.com

AUSTRIA
Frauen in Schwarz

Vienna

Facebook: facebook.com/fraueninschwarzwien
Email: fraueninschwarzwien@gmail.com

BELGIUM

Leuven

Email: marianne.vandegoorberg@telenet.be
Facebook: https://www.facebook.com/wib.leuven

COLOMBIA

Mujeres de Negro/Ruta Pacifica

Website: https://rutapacifica.org.co/wp/mujeres-de-negro/
Email: comunicaciones@rutapacifica.org.co
www.instagram.com/rutapacificam/?hl=en
Twitter: @RutaPacificaM

DENMARK

Copenhagen

Website: http://www.kvinderisort.dk
Email: Gerd Gottlieb gerd.gottlieb@outlook.dk
Tel: +45 20948744

Skanderborg

Email: Margit Andersson, margitandersson@hotmail.com
Tel: +45 24463438

Skive

Email: Solvejg Sieg Sørensen, sieg.moerch@gmail.com
Tel: + 45 23315971/97597160

FINLAND

Email: mariannex@hotmail.com
Leena Eräsaari, leena.erasaari@gmail.com
Tel: +358 040 8367738

FRANCE
Femmes en Noir

Lyon
Website: http://femmesennoirlyon.free.fr

Montbrison
http://femmesennoirmontbrison.over-blog.com/
Email: mlbousquet@free.fr

GERMANY
Frauen in Schwarz

Bonn
Email: Ifz.bonn@t-online.de

Bremen
Contact: Dr. Sabine Wedel Tel +49/ (0)421-70 70 94;
Claudia Hanses Tel +49/(0)421 – 725 72

Freiburg
Email: frauen-in-schwarz-freiburg@posteo.de

Hamburg
Website: https://friedensfrauenhh.blogspot.com/
Email: Irmgard Busemann Ibucccfis@gmail.com

Magdeburg
Contact: Hanna Maser Tel.: +49 / (0)391 – 53 46 270 Susanne
Berger Tel.: +49 / (0)391 – 40 05 461

INDIA

Website: https://vimochana.co.in/
Email: celinejaya.2010@gmail.com

ISRAEL

Haifa

Email: Orly Nathan, gamilaganani@gmail.com
Tel: +972-52-3431093

Tel Aviv

Contact: dafna.kaminer@gmail.com,
phone +97237192341
P.O Box 9013, Jerusalem, 91090 Israel

ITALY
Donne in Nero in Italia

Email: Renata La Rovere renatalarovere@libero.it
Blog: http://donneinnero.blogspot.com/ Il blog delle Donne in Nero
dell'Italia
English version of the Women in Black, Italy blog
Archive site to 2013: http://wibitaly.blogspot.com/
Archive site to 2013: https://www.blogger.com
profile/12778603772891149373

Bologna

Email: donneinnero.bo@gmail.com
Facebook: https://www.facebook.com/people/
Donne-in-nero-Bologna/100064456639391/

Padua/Padova

Email: donneinnero1.padova@gmail.com

Parma

Email: donneinneroparma@gmail.com
Facebook: https://www.facebook.com/donneinneroparma/

Piacenza

Facebook: https://www.facebook.com/Fuori-la-guerra-dalla-storia-Donne-in-nero-Piacenza-108986440757052/

Ravenna

Website: https://casadelledonneravenna.wordpress.com/donne-in-nero-ravenna/

NETHERLANDS
Vrouwen in het Zwart

Amsterdam

Email: Amsterdam@vrouweninhetzwart.nl;
info@vrouweninhetzwart.nl
Website: http://www.vrouweninhetzwart.nl
https://www.vrouweninhetzwart.nl/acties.htm

Groningen

Contact: Janny Beekman, tel. +31/(0)595-57 25 95
Email: Groningen@vrouweninhetzwart.nl
Vigil homepage: http://www.vrouweninhetzwart.nl

Haarlem

Email: haarlem@vrouweninhetzwart.nl
Vigil homepage: http://www.vrouweninhetzwart.nl

Maastricht

Contact: Frances Scarrott, tel. +31/(0)6-11 30 74 10
Email: maastricht@vrouweninhetzwart.nl
Vigil homepage: http://www.vrouweninhetzwart.nl

Utrecht

Contact: Tienta Verlegh, tel. +31/(0)30-24 13 646
Email: utrecht@vrouweninhetzwart.nl
Vigil homepage: http://www.vrouweninhetzwart.nl

SERBIA
Žene u crnom

Beograd/Belgrade

Email: zeneucrnombeograd@gmail.com
Website: http://www.zeneucrnom.org

SOUTH AFRICA

Contact: Lameez Lalkhen Llakhen@uwc.ac.za
Tel: 0027 21 9592027

SPAIN
Mujeres de Negro

Castelló

Tel. + 34 964 52 00 93
Email: VAscensio@comcas.es
Website: https://www.facebook.com/LiceuDeDones/

Madrid

Email: mdnmadrid@mujerpalabra.net
Blogspot: http://mujeresdenegromadrid.blogspot.com.es/

Seville

Website: https://sevilla.womeninblack.org/
Email: Nadia Harou, nadiaharou@gmail.com

Toledo

Twitter: https://twitter.com/MujeresNegroTo
Facebook: https://es-es.facebook.com/mujeresdenegrotoledo

Valencia

Email: Irene Cohen irenecohen@hotmail.com

UK

ENGLAND

Bradford
Email: joycerobertshaw@gmail.com
Facebook: Women in Black Bradford
Twitter: WomeninBlack_Bradford;

Cambridge
Email: tajzareenok@gmail.com

Leeds
Facebook: https://www.facebook.com/groups/
womeninblackleeds/about
Email: Devorah or Tricia — Leedswomeninblack@gmail.com
Tel: 0044 113 2888862

London
Email: WiBinfo@gn.apc.org
Twitter: @WiB_London
Facebook: https://www.facebook.com/womeninblack.london/
Vigil homepage: http://london.womeninblack.org/

Oxford
Email: Carol Stavris, carolstavris@gmail.com

Portsmouth
Email: Sarah Coote, slcoote@yahoo.co.uk

SCOTLAND

Edinburgh
Email: jbenvie@yahoo.co.uk
Facebook: https://www.facebook.com womeninblackedinburgh/

URUGUAY

Montevideo
Contact: Jenny Escobar Iglesias, Tel: + 598 (0)99921415
Email: mujeresdenegrouruguay@gmail.com
Facebook: https://www.facebook.com/mujeres.uruguay/
Twitter: @MdNuruguay

USA

CALIFORNIA

Bay Area
Email: bayareawomeninblack@yahoo.com; jberlowitz331@gmail.com; etzart@gmail.com

Berkeley
Email: wibberkeley@yahoo.com;
Marge Fouda: foudamc@yahoo.com; marinapizza@hotmail.com

Mendocino coast
Email: ldennis@mcn.org

San Francisco
Email: katrap@mindspring.com;
Judith Mirkinson mirk2@comcast.net

Sebastopol
Email: Alicia Sanchez, balicias@att.net

INDIANA

Angola
Email: lillianstoner@aol.com

Indianapolis
Email: judith_a_king@hotmail.com

MARYLAND

Baltimore
Email: wibbaltimore@peacepath911.org

Frederick
Email: wibfrederick@gmail.com

MICHIGAN

Detroit
Email: wibdetroit@gmail.com
Facebook: \https://www.facebook.com/pages
Women-In-Black-Detroit/1414825072097546

NEW MEXICO

Santa Fe
Contact: Margaret Kuhlen; please text +1 505 231 1733

NEW YORK

New Paltz
Email: Rosalyn Cherry roscherry@aol.com

Union Square
Email: Sherry Gorelick sherrygorelick@rcn.com

OREGON

Portland
Email: barbgalv@yahoo.com

TENNESSEE

Knoxville
Email: knoxvillewomeninblack@gmail.com
Facebook: https://www.facebook.com/WiBTennessee

WASHINGTON STATE

Indianola, Kitsap County
Contact: janicegutman@gmail.com

Seattle
Homelessness Remembrance Project, founded by Women in Black in 2000. Women in Black silent witnessing vigils are held whenever we learn a homeless person has died outside, in a public place, or by violence in King County.
Website: https://homelessremembrance.org/
Email: wheelorg@yahoo.com

Information on Women in Black groups from www.womeninblack.org (accessed 29.1.2023). Please check website for up-to-date information as groups and contact information may change over time.

Other organisations mentioned in the text

Action Atomic Weapons Establishment
Website: https://actionawe.org/

Aldermaston Women's Peace Camp
Facebook: https://www.facebook.com/people
Aldermaston-Womens-Peace-Camp/100064870410843/

Bat Shalom
Website: www.batshalom.org

Campaign for Nuclear Disarmament (CND)
Website: https://cnduk.org/

Campaign Against the Arms Trade (CAAT)
Website: https://caat.org.uk

Centro di Documentazione delle Donne
Website: https://centrodelledonne.women.it/

Cities of Peace
Website: www.internationalcitiesofpeace.org

El Taller
Website: https://orgs.tigweb.org/foundation-el-taller

Extinction Rebellion
Website: https://rebellion.global/

FiLiA
Website: https://www.filia.org.uk/

Hands Across the Divide
Website: https://www.annalindhfoundation.org/members/
hands-across-divide

ICAN (International Campaign to Abolish Nuclear Weapons)
Website: https://www.icanw.org/

Isha l'Isha (Woman to Woman)
Website: http://isha2isha.com/

Jewish Women's Committee to End the Occupation of the West Bank and Gaza
https://riseupfeministarchive.ca/activism/organizations/jewish-
womens-committee-to-end-the-occupation-of-the-west-bank-and-
gaza-jwceo/

Madres de la Plaza de Mayo
Website: http://madres.org/

Medica Women's Therapy Centre, Bosnia and Herzegovina
Website: https://medicazenica.org/

Mujeres que Crean (Women who Create)
Website: https://www.mujeresquecrean.org/

New Profile
Website: https://newprofile.org/

Peace Now (Shalom Achshav)
Website: https://peacenow.org.il/

Redepaz
Website: http://redepaz.org.co/

Society Without Violence NGO
Website: http://swv.am/index.php/en/

Stop Ecocide
Website: https://www.stopecocide.earth/

Trident Ploughshares
Website: https://tr/identploughshares.org

Vamos Mujer
Website: https://vamosmujer.org.co/sitio/

Vimochana — Forum for Women's Human Rights
Website: https://vimochana.co.in/

Women for Women Political Prisoners
Website: http://wofpp.org/

Women's International League for Peace and Freedom
Website: https://www.wilpf.org

Women Living Under Muslim Laws (Femmes Sous Lois Musulmanes)
Website: https://www.wluml.org/

Women's Support Network
Website: https://wsn.org.uk/

Zamir.net (for Peace.net)
Website: www.peacenet.world

(Other organisations websites accessed 1.12.2022)